Journey of Discovery

Building a Classroom Community Through Diagnostic-Reflective Portfolios

Ann M. Courtney
American International College
Springfield, Massachusetts, USA

Theresa L. Abodeeb
Ludlow Public Schools
Ludlow, Massachusetts, USA

INTERNATIONAL
Reading
Association

800 Barksdale Road, PO Box 8139
Newark, Delaware 19714-8139, USA
www.reading.org

The International Reading Association attempts, through its publications, to provide a forum for a wide spectrum of opinions on reading. This policy permits divergent viewpoints without implying the endorsement of the Association.

Director of Publications   Joan M. Irwin
Editorial Director, Books and Special Projects   Matthew W. Baker
Special Projects Editor   Tori Mello Bachman
Permissions Editor   Janet S. Parrack
Associate Editor   Jeanine K. McGann
Production Editor   Shannon Benner
Editorial Assistant   Tyanna L. Collins
Publications Manager   Beth Doughty
Production Department Manager   Iona Sauscermen
Art Director   Boni Nash
Supervisor, Electronic Publishing   Anette Schütz-Ruff
Senior Electronic Publishing Specialist   Cheryl J. Strum
Electronic Publishing Specialist   Lynn Harrison
Proofreader   Charlene Nichols

Project Editor   Shannon Benner

Library of Congress Cataloging-in-Publication Data
Courtney, Ann M., 1952-
    Journey of discovery : building a classroom community through diagnostic-reflective portfolios / Ann M. Courtney, Theresa L. Abodeeb.
        p. cm.
Includes bibliographical references and index.
    ISBN 0-87207-291-6
    1. Language arts (Elementary)—United States—Evaluation—Case studies. 2. Portfolios in education—United States—Case studies. 3. Students—Self-rating of—United States—Case studies.   I. Abodeeb, Theresa L., 1969–   II. Title.
LB1576.C738   2001
372.127—dc21

                                                                                                                          2001000846

Contents

Preface

his book shows elementary teachers how to establish communities of readers and writers who are engaged in defining and refining their own literacy processes. It advocates for both students and teachers to think constructively about classroom literacy practices through the use of diagnostic-reflective portfolios—the result of a process of collection and reflection in which teachers and students collaborate to demonstrate a learner's growth over time.

This is the story of our journey of discovery through a research study that took place for more than 5 years in a second-grade classroom. During that time, we came to understand how classroom literacy practices affect students' literacy development, and how particular assessment practices can be used to lead students to important reflections about their success as readers and writers.

Our purpose for sharing our experience is multidimensional:

- to increase teachers' awareness of the value of using an array of literacy assessments,

- to help teachers understand the importance of establishing a literacy learning community,

- to encourage teachers to reflect on and respond to an array of assessments,

- to provide theory and practical application on why it is important to include diagnosis and reflection in portfolios, and

- to provide an in-depth look at an individual student's diagnostic-reflective portfolio.

We believe our findings can help teachers construct meaningful assessment practices that reveal a close look at the processes that take place during literacy learning. This information can also help refine literacy teaching practices, which ultimately convey the belief systems that shape readers' and writers' development.

Our Story

Ann is Director of Reading and Early Childhood Education at American International College in Springfield, Massachusetts. She is a member of the School Committee in the city of Northampton and a past president of the Massachusetts Reading Association.

Theresa is a reading resource teacher at East Street School in Ludlow, Massachusetts, USA. She is a doctoral student in the Language, Literacy, and Culture program at the University of Massachusetts, Amherst, where she teaches an early childhood reading-writing course. Additionally, she is an adjunct faculty member and Director of the Summer Reading Clinic at American International College in Springfield, Massachusetts.

We met and began this project when Theresa was a beginning graduate student at American International College. Our investigation of diagnostic-reflective portfolios began in the fall of 1992 as part of an independent study on literacy assessment practices. This study arose from the frustration that Theresa and other beginning teachers experienced in search of meaningful assessment practices that reflected the literacy learning they saw taking place in their classrooms.

We agreed that Ann would visit Theresa's second-grade classroom as a participant-observer several times a month to examine the daily teaching and learning that occurred and to become a member of the classroom community. When visiting Theresa's classroom, Ann participated in all aspects of the learning community. She frequently engaged in reading conferences with students and conducted assessments such as running records and interviews. We met for several hours after each visit to discuss the learning that took place and to plan future literacy events.

Our discussions centered on theory and practice, learning and process. We sought ways to evaluate the literacy of children through methods that were meaningful, accurate, and complete. As teachers we shared the same holistic theory of the reading and writing process. We had strong backgrounds in miscue analysis, and we believed in looking at the strategies readers and writers use to construct meaning. We shared a strong commitment to using children's literature, as well as reading and writing workshops.

Our goal of improving literacy assessment practices led us to investigate portfolio use in the classroom. We believed that much was lacking in portfolios as we had seen them used. We did not want to focus on portfolios that would demonstrate only children's best work, but portfolios that would demonstrate growth and learning over time. We desired to learn about our students' literacy development through their portfolio construction; in turn, we expected our students to learn about their own literacy development through this process. We also hoped that the students would become aware of their own learning, understand how to make the most of their strengths, and learn to use strategies to improve areas of need. Together we reviewed the literature on portfolio assessment, set goals, and began to take students through the process of constructing what we call diagnostic-reflective portfolios.

Organization of This Book

Chapter 1 highlights the theoretical understandings that serve as the foundation for our beliefs about literacy and assessment practices. This chapter also defines diagnostic-reflective portfolios and discusses why they are beneficial tools for literacy assessment.

Chapter 2 explains how the literacy learning community was established in Theresa's second-grade classroom, and how she introduced portfolios to her class.

Chapter 3 details the process of diagnosing students with an array of assessment tools. This chapter includes discussion and examples of the various assessment pieces that we used in constructing diagnostic-reflective portfolios. We also discuss goal setting as an important part of the process for constructing diagnostic-reflective portfolios and as the bridge for combining diagnosis and reflection.

Chapter 4 defines and outlines the process of reflection—perhaps the most important thing to help us grow as educators. Here we detail how students were engaged in the reflecting process and how this process shaped a reader-writer's development.

Chapter 5 demonstrates how one reader-writer evolved from September to May. It provides examples of her reflections, growth, and development. A case study highlights diagnostic-reflective portfolios as an effective tool for meaningful assessment.

Finally, Chapter 6 summarizes the process of diagnostic-reflective portfolio assessment. We return to the notion that diagnostic-reflective portfolios are extremely valuable tools for assessing student literacy learning, and that they ultimately convey the practices, values, and beliefs of a classroom literacy learning community.

This book also includes an afterword of our personal reflections and an appendix of sample forms that can be used in students' diagnostic-reflective portfolios.

We invite you to join us and embark on your own journey of discovery. We also encourage you to share these insights with the larger community of concerned literacy educators and researchers, so that together we can redefine literacy learning and assessment practices in the 21st century.

AMC, TLA

Acknowledgments

We wish to convey our sincere thanks to our families. The influence, care, and thoughtfulness of Ann's husband, Richard, and children, Matthew and Elyse, have profoundly shaped her life and interests. We also thank Theresa's family and friends, especially her parents, sister, grandfather, and roommate, Roger, for their patience and understanding. We owe them all a special debt of gratitude for their emotional support during the many days and hours we devoted to this book.

We also thank American International College and Ludlow Public Schools for providing a foreground for quality educational practices and research on teaching and learning. We appreciate the helpful suggestions made by Diane Davitt, Eva Goldstein, and Kristin Cameron—dynamic teachers who helped us get this project off the ground and whose work has continued to influence our teaching and research.

A special debt of gratitude goes to the children, families, and faculty at East Street School, who have graciously shared their lives, their classrooms, and their work with us. Thanks go to Kathy Robar, Kathy Williamson, Pat Gelinas, Mabel Kornacki, Mary Elkas, Sue Loizzo, and Jill Barnes—whose commitment to the use of portfolios in their classrooms has validated our work and research—and to Principal Al Cauley, whose never-ending support, humor, and professional commitment kept us going.

We would also like to acknowledge Ben Gelinas's contribution with gratitude.

Chapter 1

Literacy Assessment and the Role of Diagnostic-Reflective Portfolios

There are many ways to interpret and find value in children's learning of language and literacy. Traditional forms of assessment, such as paper-and-pencil tests, focus on language and literacy as objects and products of learning. However, as the culture of schools has shifted in the last several decades, many teachers have found that traditional methods do not meaningfully assess the learning they see taking place in their classrooms. This conflict has led educators to call for more comprehensive assessment procedures that incorporate a wide range of processes and products that are regularly practiced and interpreted in classrooms (see Anthony, Johnson, Mickelson, & Preece, 1991; Genishi & Dyson, 1984; Goodman, Goodman, & Hood, 1989; Harp, 1996; Murphy, Shannon, Johnston, & Hansen, 1998; Rhodes & Shanklin, 1993; Valencia & Pearson, 1987; Wilde, 2000). Murphy et al. (1998) state,

> Since the 1980's, a wide range of alternative assessment initiatives have been developed. These have attempted to answer some of the critiques of the past by incorporating, for example, more texts, a greater similarity of tasks to those of school or real life, and more variety in response modes, but the evidence that these reform efforts have offered is also fragile.... This new move in assessment may lead to a more pervasive understanding that evidence is tenuous, non definitive, and open to interpretation. The goal is to put in place procedures that recognize this fact and to work to create defensible portrayals of reading. (p. 7)

Although the need for alternative assessment procedures is widespread, the implementation of these procedures highly depends on the theories and experiences of the classroom teachers who are defining them. Teachers have a central role in the assessment of literacy. They are responsible for the structure of the literacy events and assessment practices in their classroom. They have the responsibility of determining what is important for students to know.

Historically, assessment has been focused on achievement and the products of learning:

> The equation of achievement with assessment is understood by students. It is something they learn as part of learning what school is about. And, as students progress throughout the grades, the importance of equating achievement with assessment becomes more obvious and profound. By the time students reach the upper elementary, junior high and senior high grades, they are likely to orient their academic behavior to assessment rather than to learning, inquiry, curiosity, or academic substance. (Bloome, 1994, p. 58)

As a result of equating assessment and achievement, students learn to value only isolated events that mark their achievements as compared to a set of prescribed skills at any given time (Benedict, 1994; Holland, Bloome, & Solsken, 1994; Holloway, 1994; Jennings, 1994; Watrous & Willett, 1994; Wilson-Keenan, 1994). To counter this problem, meaningful, authentic assessment tools should look at students' language and literacy learning in a multifaceted way that not only brings to light an evaluation of the products of learning, but also looks at the processes and strategies students use to become more proficient in their own learning.

While trying to define our own struggle with assessment and classroom literacy practices, we had to examine our theoretical understandings of how we saw literacy learning in the classroom. Our theories have been heavily influenced by a sociopsycholinguistic perspective on reading and writing (see Edelsky, Altwerger, & Flores, 1991; Goodman, 1967, 1986; Halliday, 1975; Holdaway, 1979; Phinney, 1988; Rhodes & Dudley-Marling, 1996; Smith, 1988, 1997; Weaver, 1994). We are proponents of miscue analysis, and we believe in looking at the strategies readers and writers use to construct meaning (see Goodman & Burke, 1972; Goodman, Watson, & Burke, 1987; Wilde, 2000). We understand that these processes take place within a social context. The teacher's role is to support learners in their efforts to negotiate and construct meaning from multiple texts by helping them become consciously aware of their learning strategies (Bloome, 1994; Cazden, 1988; Vygotsky, 1986).

Our goals in constructing a literacy program were to

- fit all of the components together to provide children with meaningful experiences with literature and the construction of their own texts,
- define what our role would be in using these experiences to support and extend their literacy learning, and
- examine how we defined assessment and evaluation.

In Theresa's classroom we strived to create an environment that would foster children's understanding of texts, each other, and their own worlds (see Courtney, 1987; Cochran-Smith, 1984; Heath, 1983; Paley, 1984; Taylor, 1983; Teale, 1982). We understood that the role of the teacher is to "assess children's reading, demonstrate effective reading strategies, provide children with opportunities to read and practice a variety of approaches to text, respond to their reading, and encourage them to reflect on their reading process orally and in writing" (Taberski, 2000, p. 6). We then began to focus on assessment and evaluation.

Assessment and Evaluation

Initially, we had numerous conversations in which we loosely interchanged the terms *assessment* and *evaluation*. We came to realize that our struggle was truly with the evaluation system that had been set up by Theresa's school to report students' progress. The system was limited to quantitative assessment procedures, and Theresa felt this left out much of the growth she witnessed every day. It provided no opportunity for her to share her daily observations.

In order to think about how we could support our teaching and the students' learning in a more meaningful way, we needed to redefine and broaden our ideas about assessment and evaluation. Slaughter (1994) states, "Language educators are wise to distinguish between testing and assessment. In technical terms, testing presents a set of assumptions and limitations that may preclude a valid assessment of language. On the other hand, the term assessment can suggest a wider range of alternatives for appraising language than testing" (p. 105).

We began to recognize that assessment was something that occurred naturally in Theresa's classroom. She often wrote extensive narratives detailing students' learning behaviors, as well as comments and questions pertaining to their language development and literacy achievements. We came to understand assessment as a wide range of observational, instructional data collected for each student over a period of time, and evaluation as the analysis and interpretation of the collected assessments.

Anthony et al. (1991) state, "Assessment is used to denote the collection of information about children and educational programs, and evaluation to convey what is involved in the process of making judgments about that information" (p. xi). The collected diagnostic data allowed us and other colleagues to revisit student progress and both inform our own teaching and set future learning goals for and with students.

However, we also realized that we still had the unresolved issue of how to report these assessments in a meaningful way. We needed to focus on how to collect and organize samples in a meaningful way that would demonstrate the learning as we saw it for each student in the classroom (Tepper & Costa, 1994). This quest led us to investigate portfolio assessment. Ultimately, we began to understand the value of reflection. We decided to construct a way to examine both our students' self-evaluations and our own observations so we could share both their growth and development with others.

Reflection

Reflection is multidimensional. It enables learners to "examine where they have been, where they are now, how they got there, and where they need to go next" (Porter & Cleland, 1995, p. 34). Hansen (1998) defines reflection as the explanations, or self-evaluations, of the artifacts students select to demonstrate their growth. The process of reflection helps students develop strategies for learning, which better enables them to generalize learning from one situation to another. As Romano (1992) notes, "It's not the portfolio that matters most...[but] the process" (p. 157). Our goal was to design a portfolio process that could be used as a reflective instrument for the student and the teacher, and as a diagnostic tool for the teacher—a diagnostic-reflective portfolio.

We came to our understanding of reflection by examining psychological definitions of metacognition. In summarizing Palincsar and Brown's work (1987), Lovitt (1989) states, "Metacognition reflects individuals' understanding of their own cognitive system—that is, the way in which they think. It indicates their knowledge of cognitive resources and the use of self regulatory mechanisms such as planning strategies, monitoring their effectiveness and evaluating those strategies" (p. 322). He also summarized Brown's earlier work (1978), defining metacognitive processes as those that include

> the identification and analysis of the problem at hand, the reflection on what one does and does not know about the situation that may be necessary for solving the problem, the designing of a plan for dealing with the problem, and the monitoring of one's progress towards solving the problem. In short, metacognitive activities are those deliberate reflections on one's cognitive abilities and activities that are concerned with self-regulatory mechanisms during an attempt to learn or solve problems. (1989, p. 38)

Our definition of reflection involves *the ability to closely examine one's own learning at any given point in time.* The search or exploration is the process that leads to self-regulation in learning. As applied to literacy, it is the vocalization of inner speech (Vygotsky, 1986) that helps both the teacher and learner to understand the point in the learning process from which to determine what strategies are necessary for greater proficiency. It encompasses language in every form—from thought to word, reading to writing. It is the way students come to value themselves as learners through understanding their own reading and writing processes. Reflection allows students to internalize, take ownership of, and apply successful strategies from one literacy situation to the next.

Theresa and I initially saw portfolios as a means to collect, display, and share samples of student work. We came to discover that assessment was not in the actual collection or display of student samples but rather in the process of teacher and student reflection and interpretation of those work samples. It was the process that students and teachers went through in reflection that enabled us to examine both our own thinking processes and those of the students, which led to more strategic teaching and focused learning. The result was an increased proficiency of student literacy development.

Scaffolding

As we began to work with the students in Theresa's classroom, it became clear that students would need some guidance as they formed their reflections. Their initial reflections were not the in-depth, meaningful demonstrations of self-awareness we had anticipated, but remained at the surface level. For example, one student wrote, "I chose to put this in my portfolio because it is good." Such a response was typical, and we quickly recognized the need to scaffold the reflections for the learners.

The term *scaffold* was first introduced by Bruner and his colleagues (Bruner, 1983; Ninio & Bruner, 1978). Cazden (1988) draws on Vygotsky's zone of proximal development (1986)—the area between what students can do alone and what they can do with another's help—and positions scaffolding as a crucial component to enabling students to become successful and independent. Scaffolding is "visible and audible support" that is "well timed and well tuned" as the adult or more competent other structures an activity in which a learner can successfully participate from the beginning. As the child's competence grows, support is gradually withdrawn—the support is both "adjustable and temporary" (Cazden, 1988, p. 107). The scaffolding allows the child to participate within his or her own zone of proximal development, and gradually dissolves as the child becomes more competent.

Diagnostic-Reflective Portfolios

The word *portfolio* means different things to different people. A portfolio can be as simple as a collection of students' best work or as complex as an alternative assessment procedure (Graves, 1992; Milliken, 1992; Tierney, Carter, & Desai, 1991). It can be used as a learning strategy (Porter & Cleland, 1995) or an elaborate test (Simmons, 1992). A portfolio may become an ongoing part of the daily curriculum or something that is used only the last week of a grading period (Bergamini, 1993; Juska, 1993; Rief, 1992). Some states and school systems mandate the keeping of individual portfolios for evaluation purposes (Green &

Lane, 1994; Tavalin, 1993). Portfolios vary with each practitioner and classroom, because once the objective of the portfolio is determined, teachers and students choose to include different samples of work and assessment tools to demonstrate different things. Thus, implementing portfolios becomes a journey of discovery for both students and teachers (Courtney & Abodeeb, 1999).

Porter and Cleland (1995) define portfolios as "a collection of artifacts accompanied by a reflective narrative that not only helps the learner to understand and extend learning, but invites the readers of the portfolio to gain insights about learning and the learner" (p. 23). Tierney, Carter, and Desai (1991) define portfolios as "systematic collections by both students and teachers [that serve] as the basis to examine effort, improvement processes and achievement. Through reflection on systematic collections of student work, teachers and students can work together to illuminate student's strengths, needs, and progress" (p. 41). Hill and Ruptic (1994) define a portfolio as "an organized collection of student work and self-reflections that helps paint a portrait of the whole child" (p. 21). They add, "Reflecting upon learning is what makes a portfolio dynamic and meaningful" (p. 21).

These definitions also apply to what we have come to call diagnostic-reflective portfolios. Diagnostic-reflective portfolios are the result of a rich collaboration between students and their teachers. The student creates the work samples, the teacher generates diagnostic assessments of the learning process, and the student and teacher collaborate to construct goals and reflect on learning strategies in order to understand and further the student's individual learning process (Courtney & Abodeeb, 1999). Eventually, this reflection empowers the students to take more ownership over their own learning, achievements, and goals because they understand their own learning strengths and needs. The learning process truly becomes student-centered because the reflection focuses each child on areas in need of attention. The aim is to balance a combination of learning, assessment, and reflection to enable students to become more aware of the learning strategies they use to construct meaning, which helps them develop proficiency in reading and writing.

Decisions about collections are highly individualized and specific to each classroom, student, and teacher. Still, diagnostic-reflective portfolios should demonstrate a balance between process and product.

Portfolios need to include jointly selected pieces that represent the collaborative efforts of both teacher and student. The portfolios should include teacher observations; diagnostic instruments such as interviews, anecdotal records, checklists, and surveys; work samples; and both student and teacher reflections.

Diagnostic-reflective portfolios provide insight into a reader-writer's development. They serve as a tool for discussing the progress students have made through direct examination of their work, and as an instrument for students to set new goals they need to consider for improvement over the year. They are a valuable tool for discussing and demonstrating with parents, administrators, and other professionals the growth that an individual child has achieved (Rhodes & Shanklin, 1993).

The collected evidence demonstrates growth and development over time. One piece or observation may open a window of understanding into the learning of an individual student; pieces carefully selected over time paint a cumulative portrait of the individual student as a growing learner. A portfolio is a multidimensional tool welded with purpose to forge a collaboration between teachers and students as they participate jointly in the learning process. The ultimate purpose is to create a comprehensive, collaborative assessment-learning tool that accurately portrays literacy growth and development.

Conclusion

The creation of a diagnostic-reflective portfolio is a cyclical process (see Figure 1). Initial diagnosis and student demonstration provide a window into literacy development. The teacher, guiding the student, scaffolds to mediate, influence, and support the strategy application of the child. As Goodman and Goodman (1990) explain, "The teacher is a kid watcher who considers not only where the pupils are but where they are capable of going in their learning" (p. 237). The child's reflection reveals the child's working understanding and how this knowledge is applied in his or her daily learning. This reflection leads to increased proficiency in reading and writing. Further diagnosis confirms whether or not instruction has been internalized and new learning has occurred. Then the teacher provides more scaffolding to help students construct further meaning and continue to apply the best strategies. A child's

FIGURE 1
The Cyclical Process of Diagnostic-Reflective Portfolios

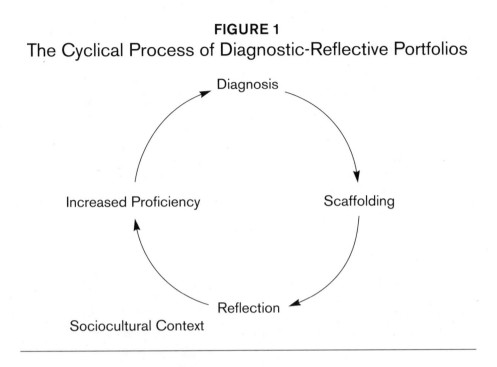

understanding of the reading and writing process is shaped by this cyclical pattern. The diagnostic-reflective portfolio is the end product that demonstrates a learner's increased proficiency over time.

This learning cycle is highly contingent on the sociocultural context in which it is fostered; building a community of learners is paramount. Learning is facilitated through the process of scaffolding. Learners become risk takers only when they feel safe to do so, and when there exists a common understanding of how the community functions, its roles and norms of operation, acceptable behavior, and what learning and practices are valued by the community itself. We discuss this building process in Chapter 2.

Chapter 2

Establishing Classroom Community

IT IS THE FIRST WEEK OF SCHOOL in Theresa's second-grade classroom. Theresa rings a bell. The students rush to the floor with their journals and form a circle. The class begins morning meeting. One by one, the students turn to the child on their right and greet them by name. This continues around the circle. As they finish greeting each other, John asks if he can share his journal first and begins to read what he has written.

stablishing classroom community is essential for the successful reflection and continued understanding of the learning processes that will become the focus of diagnostic-reflective portfolios. As Smith (1988) notes, the classroom environment must include demonstrations, engagements, and sensitivity. He defines sensitivity as "the absence of any expectation that learning will not take place or that it will be difficult." Children need to be actively engaged in and open to literacy learning. In Theresa's second-grade classroom, learning was expected to take place on a regular basis, and students began to understand learning as a process of constructing meaning. The students spent each day immersed in authentic literacy events from which they had the opportunity to continually construct meaning—individually and as a community. As Rhodes and Shanklin (1993) emphasize, "Students need to read and write in situations where they construct meaning for purposes beyond instruction and evaluation" (p. 54).

The Collaborative Classroom Setting

Theresa's classroom provided a warm environment that encouraged learning. Angled across the right side of the room, the children's desks were clustered together in groupings of four, creating small tables to enhance collaboration and discussion. The far left-hand corner served as the morning meeting area. This was dominated by a large, rattan chair used by the teacher and the children as an author's chair. Nearby, a table was covered with the themed books the children were currently exploring. A child had labeled the themed table with an illustrated poster: "We're all different—Let's Celebrate!" Another corner contained a sink, cabinets, and a work table that also served as the writing and editing table. This area contained a crate of dictionaries, spellers, and a thesaurus, as well as different kinds of paper, pens, pencils, markers, correction fluid, scissors, tape, and paste. There was also a listening station and a computer area. One door exited onto a pleasant courtyard and was surrounded with attractive display cases filled with picture books. Colorful cushions and pillows invited readers to sit or lay to enjoy reading or quiet moments. Across the window sills were bookcases and milk crates filled with more books, as well as two milk crates to collect the work samples for the children's portfolios. Theresa's desk was stacked with books and papers and was employed more as a receptacle than as a work area.

The room was also a print-rich environment. Each child's desk contained a recipe box filled with word bank cards. Theresa posted the rules of the classroom, which she had constructed with the children in a shared writing exercise. In the meeting area, the morning's message was posted on a chart stand, an easel displayed a Big Book, and a poem hung from the blackboard. Additional poems and chants appeared on the walls and bulletin boards. In the front of the room, a chart was labeled, "What do you do when you come to a word you don't know?" It was evident that Theresa and the children had been problem solving their responses, listing appropriate strategies for meaning construction. A wide assortment of the children's work was displayed everywhere. This was a fluid, flexible space that could accommodate the activities of the moment.

A Community of Learners

Theresa strived to develop a community in which shared ownership and a sense of belonging were priorities. All of the students were expected to participate, and all were encouraged to share their particular ways of knowing, so that the diverse possibilities for thinking and learning became clear to everyone. Children grew to value themselves as learners and respected each other through the activities that occurred within the community. Theresa honored differences and celebrated diversity. Within the community, children understood that they were valued as members regardless of class, race, gender, or ability. She talked to the children about what they would see and hear in the classroom regarding norms for respect, cooperation, listening, participating, sharing, and kindness. "Listening and looking at the speaker" were important rules in this classroom, allowing each child to demonstrate his or her cooperation and respect for classmates.

Theresa also devoted a great deal of time to establishing the classroom routines and procedures that would allow children to work independently throughout the school year. Together, she and the students established rules for the classroom and revisited them as necessary.

Literacy events such as reading to each other, discussing strategies and processes, celebrating authors, responding to literature, and becoming writers were daily occurrences within the community. Children learned to become independent thinkers who treasured their work, reflecting on their learning daily in a variety of ways. Celebrations of learning were important for the children to see, understand, and value the strategies they used. This reflection on their present learning allowed them to set literacy learning goals for the future. Through shared reading and writing, oral discussion, and problem solving, the students learned to respect and care about one another and to see the importance of each learner in the community. This membership encouraged students to take risks and consistently move forward in their literacy learning.

Fostering this community of learners was a long and arduous task. Like Harwayne (1993), Theresa believed that this initial work establishing community needed to be "joyful and spirited and celebratory" (p. 9). Theresa wanted her students to gain from her the passion and enthusiasm she felt about language, reading, and writing. She wanted the classroom community to be as meaningful for them as it was for her.

Theresa learned to trust that with the right framework, these meaningful experiences for the students would happen. Most important, she learned to trust the students, who eventually gained the self-control necessary for independence and free choice. By October, this cohesive, caring community was beginning to gel, and children were assuming more responsibility for their own behaviors and learning. It was clear that the many hours Theresa had invested in modeling, discussion, role-playing, and collaboration had been time well spent.

By November, it seemed Theresa's class was on automatic pilot. This became evident to Ann one mid-November day when she was in the writing center doing a running record with a student. Her back was to the class as she coded the student's reading of a book. Another child had taken sick, and Theresa left with the child for the nurse's office. Ann never knew Theresa was gone. The children were so intent on their own work that the classroom ran itself. Getting the class to this point had been a slow, time-consuming process of modeling, discussion, role-playing, and collaboration. It was time well spent, allowing Theresa the independence to work with individuals and small groups in order to assess and observe their progress.

To further strengthen the classroom community, Theresa read picture books daily to the children. She read books about which she cared deeply. In the beginning weeks of school, she selected books in which the characters were accepted, cared for, and nurtured to help her students develop a trust in each other and become comfortable enough to take risks. She read *Building a Bridge* by Lisa Shook Begaye, a story about a Navajo girl who finds friendship and acceptance on the first day in a new school. She also read *Angel Child, Dragon Child* by Michelle Maria Surat, in which a young child finds acceptance and tolerance. Theresa shared *Peach and Blue* by Sarah Kilborne and *Amos and Boris* by William Steig because both books tell the story of true friendship, cooperation, and loyalty. She read Eric Carle's *A House for Hermit Crab* to demonstrate helping relationships. With *Oliver Button Is a Sissy* by

Tomie dePaola and *Monster Mama* by Liz Rosenberg, she modeled stories about overcoming bullying and finding one's own self-worth.

Theresa also incorporated books about special relationships: *Wilfrid Gordon McDonald Partridge* by Mem Fox and *Chicken Sunday* by Patricia Polacco. She read stories about how different kinds of people learned to get along: *Old Henry* by Joan Blos, *Chrysanthemum* by Kevin Henkes, and *Crow Boy* by Taro Yashima. She read stories that contained universal truths like *Alexander and the Terrible, Horrible, No Good, Very Bad Day* by Judith Viorst and *Miss Rumphius* by Barbara Cooney. After each reading, the children openly participated in discussion about cooperation, friendship, and the respect and celebration of each other's sameness and differences. The books and discussions helped to foster a caring, nurturing, supportive community.

Theresa began each school day with a morning meeting. In the first part of this meeting, students were encouraged to share events in their lives that were important to them. This time provided an opportunity for students to get to know one another outside of learning events in the classroom. It was also a time when students modeled, respected, and learned to trust one another. During this sharing period, students openly discussed their strengths with classmates, while differences were set aside and peer relationships strengthened. As Roller (1997) notes, "Because it is a time for talking, there are no right or wrong answers and the children are the experts on the topics they introduce. It is a time when their competence is spotlighted" (p. 16). This kind of risk-free sharing had great importance and influence in achieving the sense of community that was vital for a reflective classroom. As O'Keefe (1996) states, "Students must trust the teacher and their peers will value their contributions, find their questions interesting and worthwhile and provide them with genuine thoughtful feedback" (p. 65).

During this time, the children decided to share their journals. Theresa often participated and sometimes observed. She gained powerful insights about her students, their interactions, and their attitudes, beliefs, strengths, and needs.

In the second part of the morning meeting, Theresa modeled shared strategy lessons to the class. She brainstormed charts and orchestrated discussions, guiding the children in their evolution as learners able to question Theresa and each other about their learning discoveries. Theresa also implemented and reinforced this metacognitive language process by using oral cloze. Oral cloze is the process of reading aloud a highly supportive text while stopping and omitting highly predictable words and allowing students to fill in with words that are semantically and syntactically appropriate. When students worked to predict an unknown word in the morning message or in a poem, Theresa brainstormed insertion possibilities with them. She focused them on the beginning sounds and asked what word would fit, make sense, and sound like language. Students chose the most appropriate response, which she then placed in the text. Then they all reread it together.

After each cloze procedure, Theresa asked the learners how they were able to determine the appropriate word. As they discussed their metacognitive thinking, Theresa wrote down each strategy they explained. Second grader Elaine summarized this experience when she said, "Oh I get it! First we see if it makes sense, then we check to see if the sounds are the same, and then when we go back and read it again—we see if it sounds like language." Theresa's aim was to make each reader-writer aware of and familiar with the language that was used to describe and practice proficient reading.

Introducing Diagnostic-Reflective Portfolios

In addition to reading children's literature and raising student strategy awareness, Theresa began discussing the concept of portfolios with her class in September. She read *Grandma's Scrapbook* by Josephine Nobisso, and discussed ways in which the children changed and grew. She also read *Seven Blind Mice* as retold by Ed Young, discussing the importance of seeing the whole picture. Simultaneously, she began to administer her preliminary assessments, which included reading interviews, running records, and anecdotal notes that reported her early observations of students' reading and writing behaviors.

Theresa asked students who had them to bring in their literacy portfolios from the previous year. She allowed them to share their portfolios with classmates, discussing how they had changed and grown as learners. She then implemented a collection process for the new year's portfolios. Theresa used milk crates with box-bottom folders for students to collect artifacts they wanted to include in their portfolios. The children had access to these collection crates at all times.

In Theresa's classroom, students periodically sorted through collected work samples. Every 2 to 3 weeks, they sorted through their folders and selected pieces they might want to include with final reflections in portfolios. Periodic sorting was important to learning the reflection process and enabled the children to become more self-evaluative. Students were allowed to take home anything that was not selected during periodic sorts. This kept communication flowing between home and school because parents were able to see ongoing work throughout the year.

The collection process involved modeling the procedure for sorting work. Students discussed with one another the reasons why they chose to include or exclude a certain piece. Theresa asked, "Should you put all of your best work in? Why or why not?" Then the class discussed this. She also asked, "When do you think you should put in some of your other work?" Part of the discussion centered on reasons the students may or may not have felt that a specific piece demonstrated what they had learned or how they had learned. Theresa routinely questioned students about their learning, asking them to recall how and why they thought learning had taken place.

Theresa also provided guidance to help students delve beneath the surface. For example, when Dan said, "I wanted to put this in my portfolio because I like it," Theresa continued to ask him what he liked about the piece and why he wrote it in the first place. The piece included a reader response to a book, and Dan finally responded that he wrote about that book because "it had been too hard and now it was just right." Theresa quickly jotted Dan's reflection on a sticky note and attached it to his response. Her probing enabled Dan to realize why he had made his selection and how he had grown.

The diagnostic-reflective portfolio process—involving teacher diagnosis, teacher and student collection of work samples, goal setting, and student reflections—was ongoing throughout the year in Theresa's classroom. These portfolios were used as learning tools and as evaluation and communication pieces, and were synthesized into final products in the last 2 weeks of each marking term.

Conclusion

Establishing a community of learners allows each child to become an independent thinker and risk taker. Children in Theresa's classroom were assured that learning and the learning process were valued. They became more comfortable with sharing and inquiry as normal, integral parts of the classroom community. The constant collaboration that took place made students better prepared to enter into the diagnostic-reflective portfolio process.

Chapter 3

Diagnosis and Goal Setting

IT IS THE SECOND WEEK OF SCHOOL in Theresa's second-grade classroom. Theresa sits on the floor conducting an oral reading interview with Madeline while the remainder of the class is buddy-reading books. Theresa and Madeline finish the interview. Madeline excitedly chooses one of the three books Theresa has selected for her to read. Madeline begins to read *Pancakes for Supper* by Cheryl Semple and Judy Juer, and Theresa codes a running record.

Diagnostic-reflective portfolios are purposeful collections of students' work that can teach us about the readers and writers in our classrooms. The information these portfolios provide can help us plan, adapt, and refine instruction and curriculum to meet our students' individual needs. During the assessment process, Theresa continued to process, collect, and compile information, which helped her form a meaningful evaluation over time. This evaluation considered the larger scope of each student's work and went beyond the limited view that traditional diagnostic instruments, such as tests, could provide.

Throughout the assessment process, Theresa looked for patterns in the strategies that each child used in constructing meaning, and then

18

helped the child recognize, build on, and expand on these strategies. Her aim was to foster the child's awareness of the strategies that he or she used well and to help the child refine the use and broaden the scope of these strategies, practicing them with Theresa's reinforcement until they became automatic. Through encouragement and praise, Theresa helped the child expand the repertoire of strategies in order to become an even more proficient reader.

Theresa evaluated her own teaching and sought additional ways to help her students. The children's understanding of their own learning—their metacognition—was also a piece of the assessment. With direction, the children continually reflected on their own learning.

In the beginning of our portfolio exploration, the focus was on using many different types of instruments to gather as much diagnostic information as possible. Thus, the students were assessed constantly. To prove that the use of portfolios was beneficial, Theresa tried out too many different and varied instruments. Checklists were developed just to have them. Interviews were designed just to have them. Theresa needed to determine which instruments were valuable and which were repetitive or less useful.

At the end of the first year of research, we came together and debriefed. Theresa strongly voiced her opinion that her second graders were being overtested. We had an in-depth, provocative discussion to decide exactly what we valued. We questioned the purpose of our data gathering. We determined that we gathered diagnostic information in order to compile a diagnostic profile on each individual child as a reader and a writer. This diagnostic profile informed Theresa about what the child thought he or she did in contrast to what the child actually demonstrated in reading and writing. Theresa used this information to focus and adjust her instruction and curriculum to meet the individual needs of the student. We came to understand that a balance between instruction, practice, and assessment is the desired result for effective literacy learning in the classroom.

With all assessments, the skills of observers are most important. It is essential to practice "kidwatching" (Goodman, 1978) in the classroom and to understand the theory of the holistic reading process. In traditional classrooms, students see assessment as demonstrating proficiency. Instead, Theresa wanted to encourage and assess her students' authentic, meaningful communication; purposeful learning; problem solving; and innovation.

Diagnosis

The goal in diagnosis is to assess how effectively a reader uses the language cueing systems in order to construct meaning. These cueing systems work simultaneously and interactively. The *semantic* cueing system refers to meaning. The reader draws on his or her knowledge of the world (schema) to construct meaning. The *syntactic* cueing system refers to the grammar, or rules of the language. Syntax includes "word order, tense, number and gender" (Goodman, Watson, & Burke, 1987, p. 26). This interrelationship of all the words contributes to the flow of the language and its syntax. The *graphophonic* cueing system refers to the letter-sound system of the language. The simultaneous interaction of these three cueing systems advances the reading comprehension of each child. Overriding these three cueing systems is the *pragmatic* cueing system, which is used consciously and unconsciously to adapt language to fit particular social contexts. Pragmatically, a teacher talks one way with a 6-year-old student and in quite another manner with a doctoral advisor. The language cueing systems interact simultaneously and have been separated here only for the purpose of definition.

In Theresa's classroom each September, there was a primary focus for the entire class that reading is enjoyable, purposeful, and should always make sense. The students learned that when their reading did not make sense, they should use the "blanking" strategy. In this strategy, children skip the difficult word and read to the end of the sentence. They then return to the problem word, look at the beginning sound, and figure out what word with that beginning sound would fit in that space, make sense, and sound like language. In this way, the children learned to use simultaneously the three cueing systems to the reading process: graphophonic, syntactic, and semantic. The focus was on metacognitive awareness, or learning how to learn.

On the first day of school, Theresa began individual files on each child that would include several assessments: interviews, running records, retelling outlines, anecdotal records, checklists, surveys, teacher reflection, and work samples. She used a notebook or file box, which made record keeping clear and accessible. This collection of data, evaluations, and observations translated into a diagnostic section for each child's portfolio.

To create a literacy profile on each child, Theresa interwove and connected all of the assessments, compared interviews to running records, and looked for demonstrations of strategies the child thought she or he employed during reading and writing. Literacy profiles on individual students were not placed in the portfolios, but were kept in a separate notebook of assessments that Theresa used to inform her instruction.

Samples of assessments along with synthesized narratives went into students' portfolios and were shared with parents. This allowed parents to further understand the nature and meaning of the assessments that were placed in the portfolios, as well as the focus for further instruction.

In the remainder of this section, assessments are discussed in order of their importance. These are the instruments the project research has shown to be the most beneficial in identifying the needs of students. Note, however, that none of these instruments are significant when used alone. It is the reflection on these assessments that, when looked at like data, reveals an authentic picture of a child as a reader and writer.

Reading Interview

At the beginning of the school year, Theresa orally administered Carolyn Burke's Reading Interview (Goodman, Watson, & Burke, 1987) to each child in her classroom. (See Reading Interview in the Appendix for an adaptation of this tool.) Theresa documented the strategies that the reader believed she or he used to decipher unfamiliar words. The interview was administered again in May or June as a post-test to measure growth in the child's understanding of his or her own reading processes. In some cases, Theresa also gave the interview in February or March if a child did not seem to be exhibiting necessary growth. She used this instrument to discover where her own teaching needed to be directed in order to help the child develop as a strategic reader.

Through the reading interview, Theresa was able to determine what cueing systems the child used and what strategies she or he employed when encountering unfamiliar words or other problems in the text. We agree with Goodman, Watson, and Burke (1987) that a child's beliefs about reading and reading instruction affect the strategies the child chooses to use during the reading process. The children's responses to the interview provided information about their view of reading and what cueing systems and strategies they thought they were using. Because this was an oral interview, children provided more in-depth information than they might have on a written interview. Theresa also probed for children to elaborate on their answers. She compared what the children said they did with what they actually demonstrated in the running record and reading conferences.

Madeline's September interview indicated that the only strategy she employed when she came to an unfamiliar word was to sound out the word or say "blank":

Madeline—September 23, 1996—7 years, 4 months—female—Grade 2

When you are reading and you come to something you don't know, what do you do?

I sound it out or say "blank."

Do you ever do anything else?

Not really.

Who is a good reader that you know?

My Dad and my Mom.

What makes them good readers?

Because when they get stuck on words they try to sound them out and they say "blank."

Do you think they ever come to something they don't know when reading?

Yeah!

When they come to something they don't know, what do you think they do about it?

They skip them and then go back.

If you knew someone was having difficulty reading how would you help them?

Sound it out.

What would your teacher do to help that person?

Tell them to predict and think about what words make sense.

How did you learn to read?

By practicing.

What would you like to do better as a reader?

Read harder books.

Do you think that you are a good reader?

Yes.

Madeline did not yet see reading as a process of constructing meaning. She relied on the graphophonic cueing system only to decode words, not to derive meaning, although she recognized that Theresa would advise her to "predict and think about what words make sense."

Madeline's May interview demonstrated significant growth in functional strategies:

Madeline—May 29, 1997—8 years—female—Grade 2

When you are reading and you come to something you don't know what do you do?

Say "blank" and then I read on and then I go back to the beginning of the sentence and try to figure out the word.

How do you figure out the word?

Try to remember if I've ever read that word before. Sometimes I skip it and go to another sentence and then I go back and see if I can read it.

Do you do anything else?

That's usually what I always do. Sometimes I sound it out, but not usually.

What types of things are you checking for when you skip it and go back?

What would make sense and sound like language. I also think about what [the characters] would do or be saying.

Who is a good reader that you know?

Steven [a fellow student] and my Mom and my Dad.

What makes Steven a good reader?

He practices every day and I do that, too, to become a really
good reader.

What makes Mom and Dad good readers?

They've been reading all of their lives.

Do you think that they ever come to something they don't know?

Yeah.

When Steven comes to something he doesn't know, what does
he do about it?

He thinks about what would makes sense; he says "blank."

Mom and Dad?

Think about what could make sense and maybe sound
out a little.

If you knew that someone was having difficulty reading, how
would you help him or her?

By seeing what could make sense, then what would sound like lan-
guage; use your strategies.

Strategies, like what?

Say "blank," sound out just a little, most of the time just sounding
out doesn't work.

What would your teacher do to help that person?

Say use your strategies, say "blank," go on and then go back and
try to figure it out.

How did you learn to read?

Practicing, starting with easy books and going to harder books.

What would you like to do better as a reader?

Read harder books, chapter books, really, really hard books.

Do you think you are a good reader?

Yes.

Why?

Because I practice at home and at school and I read a lot.

Madeline was now relying on many different strategies to construct
meaning. She clearly understood the blanking strategy and no longer

overrelied on the graphophonic cueing system. Madeline had grown immensely as a reader and better understood the reading process. Her running records corroborated her interviews.

The reading interview was used in the diagnostic-reflective portfolio to give Theresa a more in-depth look at students' understanding of their own reading processes and a glimpse at their reading histories. This information was important when tied to running records because it directly informed Theresa's instruction and helped her to meet instructional objectives for each student.

Running Records and Reading Miscue Inventories

In September, Theresa also assessed each student with a running record (see Clay, 1985). Running records allowed her to record oral reading behaviors and strategy use over an extended period of time. Troubled readers also received a Reading Miscue Inventory (see Goodman, Watson, & Burke, 1987). Miscues are the unexpected responses a reader makes while reading text (Goodman, 1973). Theresa analyzed each miscue to see how it changed, enhanced, or disrupted the meaning of the written text. The goal in using either of these instruments was to gain insight into the reading process and to analyze the oral reading of each student. The focus in these assessments was on the patterns of miscues that had occurred. The patterns were analyzed to assess the cueing systems and strategies that the reader was using.

Goodman, Watson, and Burke (1987) state,

> Once teacher/researchers understand, through examination of the reading process, that miscues reflect the reader's development, the reader's language system, and the reader's interpretations of meaning and context, then miscues can become a window through which much can be discovered about the individual reader as well as about the reading process. (p. 10)

Oral reading serves as a window to a child's thinking about reading, the use of language cueing systems, and the range of strategies used. This window helps the teacher to plan a supportive literacy learning environment.

All that Theresa needed for a running record was a text, a piece of blank paper, and a pencil or pen. For the initial running record, she selected an appropriate text for the child to read, a whole story that was meaningful. She would select a text that was slightly more difficult than usual and with which the child would make some miscues. For subsequent running records, the child would be directed to select a "just right" text.

To begin, Theresa explained that the child must read the text aloud with no assistance, and that the child should read the story as if no one else were present. She also explained that when the child finished reading the text, he or she would be asked to retell the story. Theresa sat next to the child so both could easily see the text. On a blank piece of paper, she coded the reading using a combination of miscue coding and running record coding. The following are codes Theresa used to interpret oral reading miscues that a reader made (see Clay, 1985; Goodman, Watson, & Burke, 1987; Wilde, 2000):

✓	= correct response
^	= insertion
o	= omission
start stir	= substitution
®	= repetitions
s-o-u-n-d	= sounding out words
©	= self-corrected the miscue

Samples of coded running records can be seen in Chapter 5 (pp. 58–59).

When possible, Theresa audiotaped the reader. Audiotapes are useful for demonstrating and discussing the strategies employed. They are also useful in parent-teacher conferences, special education evaluations, and other team meetings. Several times during the year in Theresa's classroom, the children audiotaped themselves and reflected on their own reading.

After reading the text, the child retold the story in as much detail as possible. Theresa wrote brief notes on what the child said and probed further by asking questions. Theresa did not introduce any information the child had not already mentioned. She thanked the child and spent time analyzing the coded running record in order to make recommendations for further instruction. She identified miscues and questioned whether they were syntactically and semantically acceptable, decided whether the miscues interrupted the flow of meaning, and noted any self-corrections. Theresa analyzed whether what the student read (a substitution) resembled the text (was graphically similar). She analyzed what strategies the child used well to keep meaning intact, and which strategies were ineffective or missing. Theresa noted any of the cueing systems on which the child was overrelying. After the retelling, judgments were made about the child's comprehension. Theresa made a qualitative analysis.

The theory underlying miscue analysis looks at the quality of the miscue rather than the number of unexpected responses, with the focus on the patterns of the miscues. Theresa did a running record on each child in September, November/December, March, and May/June. She performed more running records or miscues on other readers depending on their proficiency and the need to further evaluate improvement.

Chrissy was a second-grade student who struggled with reading. An analysis of her running records demonstrates how the gathering of information helped Theresa plan instruction that positively affected Chrissy's literacy learning.

Chrissy's running record of September 9 demonstrated that her reading was choppy and labored. Chrissy attempted to sound out every word she did not know, relying heavily on the beginning letters. She made no attempt to use the pictures for help. She was highly under-predictive (see Phinney, 1988), seeing reading as an exact process. She relied too heavily on the graphophonic cueing system, and took no risks to use any other cueing system. The reading became so labored that Theresa stopped Chrissy in order to instruct in the blanking strategy and use of semantic cues.

In her reading interview of the same day, Chrissy said that when she came to something she did not know, she said "the first two letters." She did not think that good readers ever came to something they did not know, and when pressed, she said she thought that they "sounded out" if they came to anything they did not know. She would tell someone who had difficulty in reading to "use their fingers to separate the words into different parts," and she imagined her teacher telling someone "the same thing."

The reading interview and running record corroborated that Chrissy used only one cueing system. Theresa began instruction in blanking, trying to make Chrissy aware of the semantic, syntactic, graphophonic, and pictorial cueing systems. The intent was for Chrissy to use her well-established graphophonic cueing system in consort with the semantic and syntactic cue systems.

As early as October 16, Chrissy's second running record demonstrated that she was making good progress. She was using some rerunning (rereading a section of text for clarification of semantics and syntax) and self-correcting strategies, and made some meaningful substitutions using the blanking strategy. Some of her substitutions changed the meaning of the text (e.g., *fish* for *fleas*). Chrissy used picture clues more effectively but, when frustrated, still relied on decoding alone.

On March 11, Chrissy was reading a much longer and more difficult text. She used her rerunning and self-correcting strategies. Sometimes Chrissy still initially attempted to sound out, which hindered her meaning construction: *stay* for *sty*, *flat* for *feathery*, *wolf* for *whoever*. In these miscues, Chrissy seemed to focus on the initial letter and then guessed wildly. However, she exhibited risk-taking behavior by frequently using the blanking strategy, reading on to gather more clues, and rerunning to self-correct. Her comprehension was now fairly good.

By June 6, Chrissy was more consistently rerunning to self-correct. She might initially sound out the word, but more often reran to construct a more meaningful substitution or to self-correct. She substituted the proper name *Putty/Putty's* for *Putter/Putter's*, which was a close match visually and in meaning. Her comprehension was good; she understood the main idea and many details. She clearly demonstrated that she was using more strategies.

In her reading interview of June 4, Chrissy responded that when she came to something she did not know, she said "blank" and later returned to "try to figure out the word and look at the picture." When probed further about other strategies, she responded, "Try to sound it out." She saw Maria, a peer in the class, as being a good reader who tried "to figure out the words and say 'blank.'" She would help someone who was having difficulty by telling them to "say 'blank' and go back and help them sound out the word, and look at the pictures." She also saw her teacher helping students by telling them to "use strategies like say 'blank,' read it over, look at the pictures and make sense, and sound it out." This was a dramatic change for Chrissy. She saw herself as a reader who enjoyed reading meaningful text by employing useful strategies along with all of the cueing systems simultaneously.

Running records were used in the diagnostic-reflective portfolios in conjunction with the reading interviews to give Theresa a clear picture of the reading processes a student used during oral reading.

Retelling Outlines

For more proficient readers, we constructed retelling outlines. (See Retelling Outline in the Appendix.) The student read the story independently, and then did an oral retelling for Theresa. Theresa marked the retelling outline as the reader noted each part. She further probed with general questions and then gave a final retelling score. Sometimes, Theresa chose to give the reader two scores, one for unaided retelling and one for aided retelling, in which she could prompt with information the student had already relayed. These two scores could be combined to obtain a total score. As Anthony et al. (1991) explain, "Retellings provide students with opportunities to synthesize, interpret; and personally recast the texts and stories to which they are exposed" (p. 87).

Retelling outlines were used in conjunction with oral reading to determine the effectiveness of a student's reading by establishing his or her comprehension.

Anecdotal Records

Continual observation is the primary factor in the ongoing assessment of day-to-day learning in the classroom. Theresa took anecdotal records on each child, which allowed her to gather rich data in a variety of literacy learning situations. To be useful, anecdotal records need to be descriptive, detailed, and specific. Power (1996) states, "Taking raw notes is the process of gathering raw ingredients. You will need time later to measure, weigh, mix, and cook what you've gathered into some kind of final product" (p. 37).

Theresa looked for specific, observable behaviors. Yetta Goodman (1978) defines these anecdotal records as "kidwatching": "The best alternatives to testing come from direct and, in most cases, informal observation of the child in various situations by the classroom teacher. Since the process itself is somewhat informal, perhaps the term 'kidwatching' is preferable to the more formal 'observation'" (p. 43). O'Keefe (1996) defines kidwatching as "a continuous, systematic look at the process of how students learn. It is taking what we know about students and turning that knowledge into effective instructional invitations" (p. 65).

In Theresa's classroom, the anecdotal records were products of kidwatching and were written on computer labels that listed the child's name and the date. During the week, Theresa moved the records to a sheet with the child's name. These sheets contained all of the anecdotal records of the particular child in chronological order. She kept these sheets in a three-ring binder, with each child's name written on a divider with colored tabs. By looking at the patterns in the anecdotal records, Theresa was able to formulate an instructional plan for individual children and to assess which students needed further observation to prevent them from falling through the cracks. Theresa also took anecdotal records by examining the students' journals, learning logs, reading logs, and work samples.

In September, Theresa's anecdotal record on Kyle stated,

> Overreliant on graphophonic, especially initial sound. Not constructing meaning. Reviewed blanking. Modeled and practiced. Do cloze. Revisit next week.

During a reading conference, Kyle demonstrated his use of the blanking strategy. Theresa noted that he seemed to have internalized that it meant looking at the first letter and guessing on the initial sound only. His miscues did not make sense; they were wild guesses that began with the same initial sound. Theresa's anecdotal record noted the observable behavior and then briefly recommended an immediate intervention plan.

In December, Theresa's anecdotal record on Madeline stated,

> Madeline responds to *Candy Corn Contest* by asking for help to choose more mystery stories. Start mystery genre. Work on writing. Pair with Jane.

When Madeline expressed her desire to read only mystery stories and to write one, too, Theresa jotted down what she observed and made a quick action plan. From her anecdotal record, Theresa understood that she was to have a discussion with Madeline and Jane on the components of mystery and to facilitate writing. In addition, Theresa wrote another label to place in her plan book:

> Mystery genre study??? Check interest with class.

Ongoing observation opens the window to students' learning and informs instruction. Kidwatching must become a daily part of teaching. Anecdotal records document each child's developing literacy and demonstrate how well the teacher understands that journey. The records enabled Theresa to design supportive environments for each child's developing literacy and frequently focused on how well the children were meeting the portfolio goals they set with Theresa.

Checklists

Spelling. Theresa also kept several checklists on her individual students. One of the checklists was on the child's movement from temporary spelling to more traditional spelling. Theresa plotted samples of a child's spelling on a checklist she devised to gauge developmental stages of spelling based on the work of Gentry and Gillet (1993). (See Temporary Spelling Evaluation in the Appendix.) As the child demonstrated spelling knowledge, Theresa placed samples next to the appropriate stage on the checklist, including the date that she took the sample. Theresa did this periodically throughout the year until the child entered the transitional spelling stage. Some second graders may not enter the transitional stage until the end of the year; for other second graders, that entry can be as early as January.

See Chrissy's Temporary Spelling Evaluation (Figure 2) for an example of how this assessment tool is used. In October, Chrissy wrote primarily in a phonetic stage, writing the letters of the sounds she heard. She used some standard spelling of high-frequency words. In March, Chrissy was still a phonetic speller, but she was moving toward a transitional stage of spelling. She demonstrated a greater reliance on the visual aspects of print. By June, Chrissy's spelling was primarily at a transitional stage, with all high-frequency words spelled conventionally on a consistent basis.

Reading. Theresa also filled out a reading checklist for each child. (See Reading Checklist in the Appendix.) This was done after conferences with the child and was informed by Theresa's running records and anecdotal records. The process enabled her to plan with the child for the most supportive instruction and to look at the child's reading on a continuum of developmental skill. Theresa used the bottom of the form for personal statements about each child. Theresa found this checklist

FIGURE 2
Chrissy's Temporary Spelling Evaluation

Name: *Chrissy*   Grade: *Gr. 2*

Date:	10/16	3/14	6/8	
Precommunicative String of letters or symbols. e.g., mrbsopnd				
Semiphonetic One-, two-, three-letter spellings. Some letter/sound correspondence. e.g., wnt – went Dg – dog				
Phonetic Close match between sounds and letters. e.g., becos – because Wot – what Sed – said	10/16 wit=went sey=saw faru=true			
Transitional Less reliance on sounds. Close to standard spelling. Greater reliance on visual aspects of print. e.g., House – house		3/14 wint = went wine = when Salmndrs = salamanders	6/8 bc eaues = because found = found thay = thay	

10/16 – Mostly phonetic sp., some standard (high frequency).
3/14 – Making a move toward transitional spelling, most high frequency words are conventional.
6/8 Mostly transitional. Making a major move toward standard spelling

beneficial in sharing with parents as they viewed the child's records and thought about the student's reading.

Writing. The writing checklist was devised by Theresa's school district to assess young learners' emergent and early writing skills. (See Writing Checklist in the Appendix.) The district hoped that this checklist would guide and refine teachers' observations of students and the writing process.

Theresa found this checklist helpful and included it as one of the assessments in each child's portfolio. She administered each child a writing prompt at the end of October, January, and March, and analyzed the writing prompt to assess the student's sense of story; recognition and use of beginning, middle, and end; introduction of characters; character development; style; plot; setting; spelling; and punctuation. (For some children, a writing prompt creates writer's block, and they are not able to demonstrate how capable they are as writers. When using writing prompts, there is a strong need to compare the prompts to the child's everyday writing in the workshop.) Theresa used the analysis of the writing prompts to complete the district writing checklist and to inform her teaching.

The spelling, reading, and writing checklists were used in diagnostic-reflective portfolios to help synthesize varied assessment tools, anecdotal records, and work samples to make reporting of progress more clear to parents and other professionals who read the portfolios. It is important to note that these checklists do not report some significant behaviors, which teachers must consider when planning instruction.

Attitude Surveys

In the beginning of the year, Theresa administered a reading attitude inventory to assess how each child felt about reading. (See Elementary Reading Attitude Survey in the Appendix.) Later in the year, the children completed a post-inventory. When they were finished, Theresa asked the students to compare how they initially felt about reading and how they felt now, based on their answers to the two inventories. Students frequently saw dramatic shifts in how they felt about their own reading. This was helpful for students and for Theresa, and was particularly influential in her assessment of reluctant and struggling readers.

Reading attitude surveys were used in the diagnostic-reflective portfolio to assess how readers' attitudes changed over time, particularly as reading proficiency increased.

Teacher Reflection

Theresa synthesized all of the diagnostic data and developed a learning profile for each child. The learning profile, kept in the diagnostic section of the portfolio, comprised interpretations of the collected diagnostic data compared to what Theresa observed the child doing in day-to-day learning. These interpretations informed her teaching and helped to foster a community that was supportive of continued literacy growth.

Analysis of diagnostic data for each child should inform both curriculum and instruction. Theresa became aware of students' strengths and needs in order to implement an action plan that could support strategic learning. The diagnostic section of the portfolio enabled her to discuss strengths and weaknesses with students, parents, and other professionals; make appropriate recommendations for instruction; assess growth on a continual basis; and compare student self-reflections (see Chapter 4) to her diagnosis and her reflection. This was the time to wed assessment and observation with learning and instruction (Johnson, 1992).

The following examples illustrate how these multidimensional assessments informed Theresa's understanding of particular students:

Theresa's Early Learning Profile of Madeline

Madeline's reading interview shows that she is using only one cueing system, the graphophonic. She further demonstrates the overuse of this cueing system in her running record.

model blanking strategy immediately

model rerunning

discuss focus on meaning

cloze exercises

guided reading

rewrite of poetry focusing on meaningful substitutions

Theresa reflected on and analyzed the diagnostic data to create a learning profile and action plan for immediate strategy instruction for Madeline.

In another situation, Theresa was confused by Ben's inability to develop as a fluent, confident reader. At group time or during a conference with Theresa, Ben was always the first one to discuss appropriate, meaningful strategies, but he failed to apply the strategies during the process of reading. Theresa wrote the following learner profile to figure out exactly what was going on. She shared it with Ben's parents so they could also understand what Ben was thinking.

Theresa's Early Learning Profile of Ben

Ben reports using blanking strategy in reading interview.

Running record—sounding out every word.

Reading conference—limited to sounding out as a strategy.

Group discussions—Ben "parrots" everything I say about meaning and blanking.

Demonstrates no meaning-getting strategies.

Not successful independently, not able to read books that he should be able to read.

Tape record Ben reading and listen to tape with him.

In a reading conference, Theresa audiotaped Ben reading a story. When they reviewed the tape together, Theresa was able to point out where Ben was losing meaning. This was a turning point. Ben was able to hear and discuss with Theresa why he was not able to construct meaning. Theresa reported that Ben cried and screamed at her in frustration, "You tell me to say 'blank,' but my mother tells me to sound it out. I wish the two of you would decide what I should do." Theresa called Ben's parents in for a conference. She explained to Ben's mother that the students absolutely use sounding out along with meaning and grammar. She further explained that it was most important for Ben to construct meaning, rather than just say words that looked a lot like the text. When Theresa explained that these mixed messages were confusing for Ben, his mother agreed to ask him to make sense first. As a result, Ben slowly internalized strategies to construct meaning successfully.

Theresa's insightful kidwatching and sensitivity helped her sense the conflict Ben was experiencing in his development as a reader. He displayed the behavior he believed Theresa expected and expressed this in his reading interview and class discussions; however, his oral reading revealed that his practice did not match his reflection. In an unobtrusive way, Theresa mediated his transactions with his environment, specifically with his parents, to stretch and extend his literacy learning capabilities. Once Theresa and his family had a meaningful dialogue about Ben's confusions, they were all able to help him. This process of diagnosis, inquiry, demonstration, and reflection led to Ben's increased proficiency as a reader. Theresa provided Ben with multiple opportunities to test out, practice, and reflect on his literacy learning behaviors. Eventually, these behaviors became internalized and operational. Thus, Ben was empowered as a learner because he owned and used his meaning-constructing strategies more independently.

Teachers must continually expand their observations and reflect on what they see in order to provide the most supportive literacy learning environments for children. Both Madeline and Ben needed to become aware of their own learning. Before they could become successful, their learning needed to become concrete and visible to themselves. Based on her own diagnosis and reflection, Theresa was able to plan a program to meet each child's needs.

Goal Setting

Portfolios are driven by the goals the children and teacher set together. The teacher's role is to guide each individual learner in setting realistic and appropriate goals. To help children develop this skill, Theresa began by asking the class to brainstorm what they thought a goal was. She wrote this language on chart paper to serve as a model of goal-setting language. Some of the children's responses were,

- A goal is something that you practice, practice, and practice until you get it and then you have a new goal.
- A goal is something that you think is hard, but over time, when you've reached your goal, you don't think it is hard anymore.

Theresa then worked with the class to brainstorm ideas about goals and she recorded them on chart paper. After the brainstorming session, she led a discussion about what specific goals students might have. Theresa asked the students, "What are the things that you might want to work on or get better at?" She then modeled the language for appropriate goal setting by paraphrasing student responses and recording them on chart paper.

Theresa elaborated on the sample goals by asking students to describe how they might specifically work on the goals. She expanded further by asking, "If you were working on your goal, what might I hear or see you doing?" Theresa recorded several responses from the group and broke them down into specific observable behaviors. Some sample goals that second graders set were,

- Get better at reading by putting in words that fit, make sense, and sound like language.
- Improve my writing by reading my drafts out loud and then changing them.
- Improve reading by reading at home and at school.
- Work on staying on task by staying in my seat and paying attention to the speaker.
- Make sure that when I work no one else is in my way.
- Get better at spelling by reading more books.

Theresa conferred with each child in the classroom, repeated the goal-setting process, and helped each student record three specific, appropriate learning goals. She wrote the goals on index cards and taped them to the child's desk. Some students became self-directed with their goals and consciously worked on them most of the time. For others, Theresa needed to help the children attend to goals and elicit reflections on how they were meeting their goals. For these learners, Theresa asked, "What is something you said you wanted to work on while you were reading? How am I going to see you do this? Can you show me an example of this before you start reading today?" This enabled the child to know what the goal was, recognize its purpose, and define a process to achieve it. Goal setting was extremely important as a strong foundation for honest self-evaluation and reflection in the future.

Students reflected on goals in diagnostic-reflective portfolios in order to further connect what Theresa and the children discussed during assessment and instruction. Reflecting on these goals empowered students to take an active role in their own learning.

Conclusion

In this second-grade classroom, assessment was part of a tightly woven web of literacy learning, literacy instruction, reflection, and analysis. Diagnostic data were gathered through interviews, running records, checklists, inventories, and critical observations. Further, Theresa analyzed and reflected on the diagnostic data in order to make children aware of their learning, and to make instructional decisions that supported children during literacy learning. She drew conclusions after similar information emerged from multiple data sources—usually teacher, student, parents, and other professionals (Rhodes & Shanklin, 1993).

To construct diagnostic-reflective portfolios, we recommend starting simply, using only a few key assessment tools that are a good match for your students. When you are comfortable, add on or refine the process as it makes sense. This will enable your own growth as a critical observer and develop your confidence in your data-gathering abilities. Assessment guides literacy learning and documents its development. Like Rhodes and Shanklin (1993), we believe that "teachers should draw on assessment information to decide how best to support students' literacy development" (p. 3).

Chapter 4

Becoming Reflective

IT IS THE THIRD MORNING OF PORTFOLIO
CONSTRUCTION in Theresa's second-grade classroom.
Students are busily sorting and discussing with each other
pieces that they will include in their portfolios. Theresa rings a
bell and calls all of the children to the carpet, asking them to
bring to her the lists of reading and writing goals that have been
taped to their desks. Theresa has already asked Steve, an
emergent reader, to demonstrate goal reflection for the entire
class. He happily takes a seat next to Theresa at the overhead
projector to discuss goal reflections while the rest of the class
eagerly sits on the floor.

In Theresa's classroom, students constructed diagnostic-reflective portfolios prior to the end of each marking period (typically three times a year). Throughout each marking period Theresa was assessing, conferencing, questioning, and modeling while students demonstrated reading and writing, collected and sorted work samples, and practiced reflections. During the last 2 weeks of each marking period students did final sorting and made decisions about what they were putting into the diagnostic-reflective portfolio. The final reflection process enabled students to review their goals and work samples, raising consciousness of the strategies they were using to become more proficient readers and writers.

Reflection is multidimensional. It requires students to form an awareness of the various strategies they use throughout the learning experience and requires a unique language for students to articulate and convey an understanding of their own learning. In reviewing Vygotsky's work, Bodrova and Leong (1996) point out, "Language enables children to reflect on their inner thought processes and makes a major contribution to the emergence of higher mental functions" (p. 60). From class discussion to setting individual goals, sorting artifacts to constructing portfolios, Theresa's students were immersed in learning experiences that naturally demanded self-reflection. In addition, Theresa provided the children with a multitude of modeling experiences with reflective language, and then asked them to practice using it for reflection, first orally and then through writing. The students' reflection, though initially difficult, developed into an automatic process and a vital part of every learning experience. It became a way of life in this second-grade classroom. Reflection in the diagnostic-reflective portfolio was used for the reader to gain insight into his or her own reading. It was through this process of reflection that students were able to revalue themselves as readers (see Goodman & Marek, 1996).

Like Porter and Cleland (1995), we believe in the power of reflection, and that it is the most valuable vehicle teachers can use; reflecting on a routine basis "can provide learners with valuable insight into their learning processes" (p. 35). Some samples of typical reflection probes we used included

What did you do to help yourself get better at _____?

How did you make sense while you were reading?

What do you think you still need to work on in writing?

What did you do when you came to a word you didn't know?

Theresa constantly found opportunities in the classroom to probe with questions like these.

In summarizing Gal'perin's (1969) and Davydov's (1986) work, Bodrova and Leong (1996) state, "In early primary grades, higher mental functions are just emerging, so children are able to perform some strategies but need contextual support or assistance to use them effectively, such as shared activities with peers or the teacher" (pp. 61–62). As a result, we designed a model in which a child volunteer sat at the overhead with Theresa's support and guidance to demonstrate the reflective process for the whole class.

Initial Reflections

When we began our research, Theresa and I naively thought all children could take a reflective stance. In the first efforts, Theresa supplied a few sentence starters that she assumed would help put children in a reflective mood. Some examples of sentence starters she used were,

I chose this piece because...

I'm proud of the way...

This shows that I...

What I still need to improve on is...

This was meaningful to me because...

I learned _____ about myself.

Through the students' responses, we quickly realized that the children were not reflective by nature. Their responses were on the surface level only. For example, Amy reflected, "I chose this piece because I did good."

During the first year, the children compiled only one portfolio in May. When we reviewed the portfolios, the students demonstrated a basic inability to reflect on their own work. They never truly took a reflective stance. We received reflective statements such as, "I've gotten better at writing" and "I've gotten good at reading." Monica wrote, "I like my writing because its neater." Cate's reflections were similar:

"I chose this piece of writing because I werked [worked] hard on it."

"I remember when I worked on it I felt happy because I coudint wate to finyis [couldn't wait to finish]."

"When I finished I smilyld [smiled]."

"Now when I read it I fell [feel] good."

"The things I did to help me write this story were use puncsouayson [punctuation]."

"The thing I want to work on with other writing pieces are write neater."

These reflections were not the meaningful, probing demonstrations of self-awareness that we had anticipated. Students were not focusing on the process of learning, the steps they went through, and the strategies they used or could use in constructing a product. They were only focusing on the product itself. We were not happy with reflection as a learning strategy at this time, although Cate was clearly happy with the work she accomplished that year. While working hard, feeling happy and good, smiling, using punctuation, and having a goal of writing neater were admirable, Cate did not indicate a metacognitive awareness that pertained to her abilities in reading and writing proficiency.

Theresa engaged students in a reading and writing workshop as a community of learners. Students were allowed to make many of their own choices in both the literature they read and the writing pieces they created. Students interacted in writing conferences and responded in literature circles with both peers and teachers. In spite of all of this, students were still not as reflective as we wanted them to be. As a result, we decided to examine students' weekly practice reflections. Students performed these reflections in a very informal manner to ensure that the opportunity to practice meaningful reflection was being provided. The routine self-evaluation was written on a chart and hung in Theresa's classroom. Frequently throughout the week, students ended their day by orally reflecting with Theresa and the other students as they sat on the rug in a sharing circle. This was one way that students regularly practiced reflection through oral rehearsal. (See Routine Self-Evaluation in the Appendix.) We decided to structure some reflective sheets that would guide the students in formulating their own reflections.

To that end, we constructed reflective sheets that asked several questions we hoped would elicit meaningful reflections. (See Book Log Reflection in the Appendix.) Theresa read the reflective sheets with the children, and then they reflected independently.

The Struggle to Generate Quality Reflections

During the second year of the research project, Mike, another second grader, responded to a Book Log Reflection in May:

1. What book did you like best? Why?
   "an elephant in the house because it's coooool."
2. What was the easiest book to read? Why?
   "Just like Grandpa it's yost ese [just easy]."
3. What was the hardest book? What did you do to help yourself read it?
   "Mr. beep I read it and blackt [blanked] it."
4. What book do you remember the most? Why?
   "just like grandpa I reda it olot [read it a lot]."
5. What book taught you the most? How?
   "The last dinosaur because it tot [taught] me about dinosaurs."
6. What are the things you want to do to become a better reader?
   "reading harder books."

The questions on the Book Log Reflection had been organized to continually prompt and probe the reader's metacognition in more detail. At this time, Mike was reflecting independently. He was beginning to understand the correlation between strategy use and proficient reading, but he still failed to write in-depth observations that related to his concepts about texts and language learning.

Mike's reflections were a result of constructing two portfolios (in December and May) in the second year of our study, versus one in the first year. We attributed this slight growth to Mike's increased practice in collecting, sorting, and reflecting on the contents of the diagnostic-reflective portfolio. At this point, although Theresa was discussing reflection more often, it was still not the focus of instruction or modeled consistently throughout the year. Mike's responses were slightly more reflective than Monica's or Cate's, demonstrating an expanded awareness of the metacognitive process, but without the deeper understanding of learning strategies. Although we saw evidence of progress with students like Mike, we were still disappointed in their overall level of reflection. Most reflections remained superficial.

While the children were elated about the growth they could recognize in themselves from September, they could not recognize what they had done to achieve that progress between September and May. As they compiled their portfolios, they knew they had gotten better, but they were not sure why. Our focus now became to teach the process of reflection in conjunction with specific learning strategies.

We recognized that students needed to understand the process of reflection and to acquire the language to discuss their own learning. In a cause-and-effect fashion, we had to demonstrate their learning to them so they could in turn demonstrate their learning through the use of reflective statements. Theresa modeled the appropriate language for both reading and writing peer conferences. She heightened the students' awareness of the types of questions that draw out specific aspects of literacy learning. The goal was always to provide students with ownership of the language, along with an understanding of their own individualized learning processes. The language of conferencing developed into a genre in and of itself. Similarly, reflection demonstrated the need to use specific language. This reinforced our understanding that reflection was not a natural process for our students. We therefore made sure that students were engaged in a great deal of oral rehearsal prior to doing written reflecting, which helped to shape the language that students used to discuss their own learning strategies.

The Zone of Proximal Development

We soon recognized that if we expected children to develop a reflective stance, it was our responsibility to provide support. We revisited Vygotsky's theory on the zone of proximal development during the second and third summer when we met to discuss ways to encourage deeper reflection. The *zone of proximal development* was a term coined by Soviet psychologist Lev Vygotsky (1986) to describe the behavior of a learner on the edge of emergence that will develop in the near future. The first level in the zone is characterized by what the child can accomplish independently and shows work at the child's lowest level of achievement; the second level is characterized by what the child can do with maximum assistance and demonstrates the highest proficiency attainable by the child. The zone continually shifts as the student gains more knowledge and experience. What the child can do with assistance one day will be what the child can do independently tomorrow. Assistance is usually in the form of social interactions with a significant other: a teacher, an adult, or a more capable peer. The interaction can also take the form of indirect help, such as working with an environment of supportive learning.

Informed by Vygotsky's theory, Theresa decided to create even more guided opportunities for students to practice reflection in the classroom. At the same time, she made plenty of time for teacher modeling to expose them to the assisted learning at the higher end of their zone of proximal development.

At this time, research on learning as inquiry by Short, Harste, and Burke (1996) influenced us significantly. This probing, this inquiring, this scaffolding was the piece that we felt had been missing in the first and second year of our research study.

Theory Into Practice

In October of the third year, Theresa and I made a presentation on diagnostic-reflective portfolios for the Massachusetts State Department of Education. Our attendees had agreed to visit the classroom to see follow-up demonstrations and the portfolio process. In preparing for this visit, Theresa and I revisited Vygotsky's zone of proximal development and formed a direct model for teaching reflection. This model, described in the "Scaffolding Reflection" section of this chapter, provided specific language for students to describe their own learning.

That year reflection permeated every layer of the classroom. Theresa helped the children create a natural reflective stance for everything they did. She taught them to question themselves constantly as they read: Does it sound like language? Does it make sense? In accordance with Vygotsky's description of the zone of proximal development, Theresa helped the children to report their learning by using language that described their learning in terms of specific observable behaviors. At the overhead projector, Theresa would work with one of the children to model reflection for the class. Together, they would discuss a piece of writing or a Book Log Reflection. Theresa's role was to scaffold the reflection by pointing out specific aspects of the child's learning processes with concrete examples of what the child did or did not choose to notice or discuss. Theresa was now providing an authentic learning experience for the class to observe.

The use of verbal scaffolding is supported by Piaget's Law of Awareness, which states that any impediment or disturbance to an automatic activity creates an awareness of that activity in the child. As the child moves to awareness, she or he expresses the process through egocentric speech (Piaget, 1955). Piaget suggested that egocentric speech does not fulfill any useful function in the child's behavior, but merely accompanies it. He further suggested that the child is not communicating with anyone. Vygotsky (1986), on the other hand, believed that egocentric speech serves as an instrument of thought—a means of seeking and planning a solution to a problem. While Piaget believed that egocentric speech disappears with egocentrism when a child approaches school age, Vygotsky hypothesized that egocentric speech evolves into inner speech as a child approaches school age. He saw egocentric speech as related to the child's interactions with the world around him or her. Vygotsky added that, for adults, inner speech represents independent thinking and has the same function that egocentric speech has in a child. Vygotsky and Piaget used the same term, but each saw it as something different. Vygotsky's theory guided our creation of the direct model for teaching reflection.

Theresa implemented classroom practices supported by these theories. During the modeling process, she directed the student to revisit a familiar and routine activity, such as a book log. She asked the child to describe the activity, then disrupted the child's thought by questioning in a reflective manner. In this way, the child transitioned from voiced egocentric speech to voiced inner speech. This, in turn, led to the awareness of thought, which, over time, directly influenced the student's reading and writing development. The child did what she or he was capable of doing and Theresa did the rest—a working example of assisted learning. Theresa and the child collaborated in the reflection process by experiencing its context. Through this interaction, the teacher gradually increased the expectations of the child's performance, lessening involvement and drawing the child into a more independent performance.

Scaffolding Reflection

Bruner (1983) and Cazden (1988) use the term *scaffold* to describe the teacher's role in assisting the child's performance as stated by Vygotsky. This scaffolding gradually lessens as the child's competence grows. Cazden points out that in fine-tuning techniques, specific instruction of this nature most often occurs between teachers and individual students. Consequently, Theresa structured her individual work with students during independent work time or while modeling the reflection process for the whole class. As the individual student and the rest of the class became more competent in their understanding of using reflective language, Theresa increased her expectations for the children's independent reflections.

By the middle of the year, most of the children were willing to come to the overhead to share openly in front of their peers. However, students always had the opportunity to pass when Theresa asked them to participate. In the beginning of the year, Theresa only included students who had a high level of confidence in their abilities or had demonstrated by volunteering that they were willing to participate in the reflection process before their peers.

The following transcript demonstrates our direct model of teaching reflection and how Theresa models it at the overhead with a second grader named Steve, and how she scaffolds his work:

Theresa: Do you think you are getting better at reading?

Steve: Yes.

Theresa: So you've been working on your goals?

Steve: Yes.

Theresa: How have you been getting better at reading?

Steve: By reading more books and practicing making more sense.

Theresa: We need to write a whole sentence. So how are we going to start that off? I have...

          [Reads goal statement. Steve and teacher read the goal statement together.]

Steve: I have been getting better at reading by reading more books and practicing making more sense.

          [Theresa repeats each word that Steve dictates as she writes.]

Theresa: How were you making sense? What were you doing to help yourself make sense?

Steve: I was putting in the word that I decided would make sense.

Theresa: [Theresa paraphrases and writes what Steve dictates.] I put in a word that made sense when I came to a word...

Steve: ...that I didn't know.

            [Theresa repeats and writes, modeling on the overhead.]

Theresa: Did you do anything else when you came to a word that you didn't know?

Steve: I tried to read the sentence over again.

            [Theresa repeats and writes.]

Theresa: Did you do anything else? Did you look at any part of the word? Did you skip the word?

Steve: I...

            [Steve shrugs his shoulders.]

Theresa: So you are telling me that when you came to a word you didn't know, you put in a word that you decided would make sense, and then you tried to read the word over again. Did you do anything else?

Steve: Tried to skip the word.

Theresa: And did that help you?

Steve: Yes.

Theresa: And it helped you be able to read more books; you said that you are reading more books. I want to tell you that I really notice you have been doing that. You have been reading a lot more books, and that also involved taking risks, trying to read more books that you didn't already know and using some of those strategies to help yourself. But, I do notice that you do something else when you read to try to make sense, something that really helps you to think about what is happening in the story or in the book. You look at something.

Steve: I look at the pictures.

[Theresa paraphrases and writes.]

Theresa: I also look at the pictures.

[Theresa addresses the class.]

And how many people still feel that is a really important strategy that they use sometimes to figure out words that they don't know?

[Many students raise their hands.]

If it helps you to make sense while you're reading, then it's a really important strategy to use. Pictures help all of us understand a story. Thank you, Steve, that was great reflecting.

As the interview began, Theresa questioned Steve to elicit a response that demonstrated a specific, observable behavior. She reaffirmed what Steve said by repeating it, and questioned him further to draw out his answer. Theresa also paraphrased what Steve said in order to give him the opportunity to hear the meaning she constructed from his response. This gave him the opportunity to accept, reject, or clarify his intentions.

If we look only at Steve's responses, we see that he was unable to articulate independently how he achieved his goals. If left on his own, Steve probably would have written, "Yes, I have gotten better at my goals." Theresa helped Steve elaborate and clarify his own responses through a scaffolding process, increasing his awareness of his own learning. The paraphrasing was a demonstration of written language that maintained Steve's language to describe his reading. He could agree, disagree, or change whatever he said.

Steve's level of response surprised us in the depth of his awareness. He recognized that because he was using more strategies and was selecting many more books, he had become a better reader. We were also excited that he was able to articulate strategies he used successfully as Theresa provided scaffolding with questions such as "What were you doing to help yourself make sense?" Because of the time she had spent kidwatching, Theresa was able to confirm and reinforce the strategies that Steve used well. She also helped him recall other strategies that may not have come to his awareness without the scaffolding process. Their discussion demonstrated to the rest of the class which strategies a good reader might use, and how these strategies help to support proficient reading. The other students acknowledged and became a part of this process as they interacted with Steve and Theresa throughout the demonstrated reflection process. Through these types of interactive demonstrations of reflection, students can reflect, discuss, become aware of, and interpret their different learning strategies.

In another modeling session, Molly worked with Theresa at the overhead while the class listened to a tape of a "just right" story that Molly had read into a tape recorder earlier in the morning. Theresa had a copy of the story on the overhead and coded the miscues from the audiotape. Molly had made the miscue *Miss Lockett made sure* for *Miss Lockett made some*. The scaffolding process was used in front of the entire class to enable Theresa, Molly, and the class to work through the miscue and to help Molly recognize the strategies she used as well as the ones she needed to remember to use in the future. Molly was seated in a chair facing Theresa and a screen next to the overhead. The rest of the students were on the floor. Here is a transcript of the session:

Theresa: Why do you think you said "made sure"?

[Molly shrugs.]

Why do you think you said "made sure"?

[Theresa turns to address class.] Why?

Carl: "Made sure biscuits" doesn't make sense.

Theresa: Right, but she didn't read it that way. She said, "Miss Locket made sure blank." She used her blanking strategy. Why do you think she said "made sure"? Oh no, did I stump you guys?

Class: No!

Theresa: What strategy was she using when she said "made sure"?

Kerry: Putting in a word that might have made sense.

Theresa: Yes, I agree with you that it might make sense up until you get to the next word.

Matt: She was sounding out.

Theresa: Are you sure? Does *sure* sound like *some*?

[Theresa sounds out *s-u-r-e* and then *s-o-m-e* and compares.]

Does it sound the same? Do they have the same letters?

Andy: Only the beginning and the end.

Theresa: Only the beginning and the ending sound are the same, so she might have been trying to put in a word that might have made sense, but "Miss Locket made sure..."

Kerry: What I think she was trying to do was put in a word that looked similar and had the same amount of letters.

Theresa: Yes, putting in a word that would look similar and had the same amount of letters. Maybe, but it also sounded...

Class: Like language.

Theresa: Yes, sounded like language. So, let's look at this [oral reading] reflection [see Figure 3]. What are all the things you did when you came to a word you didn't know?

Molly: I blanked.

Theresa: I said "blank." [Theresa writes on overhead.]

Molly: And after, when I was done with the sentence, I went back and see and tried to make sense when I came to a word I didn't know.

           [Theresa repeats everything Molly stated and writes it on the overhead.]

Theresa: You were checking to make sure it made sense, made sure it sounded like language, made sure it would fit, and checked for the sounds. So, you were really doing all of those things.

Molly: Yes.

Theresa: When you used this strategy, it did what?

Molly: It helped me to try to figure out the word and...

FIGURE 3
Molly's June Oral Reading Reflection

Name   *Molly*   Date   *6-4*

Title *The robber pig and the gingger Beer.*

While I was reading, I *said blaaHK and after when*
I was dome with the sentence I went Back
and tried to make sense Sound
_____.

When I came to a word I didn't know, _____
_____
_____ .

When I used this strategy, it *helpen me try to*
figure out the Word and make
sense.
_____ .

Next time I will *try to picture the word in my*
head and think about what makes sense,
_____ .

This book was too hard, too easy, or just right. (Circle one choice.)
_____

Theresa: When I used this strategy it helped me figure out the word and.... What's the goal when you are reading? You want to know what?

Molly: It...it...it makes sense.

Theresa: You want to know if it makes sense because you want to know what is happening in the story. You are trying to understand the story right?

Molly: Yes.

Theresa: So, when I used this strategy it helped me to try to figure out the word and...

Molly: Made sense.

Theresa: And made sense. Next time, I will...

Molly: Next time, I will try to picture the word.

Theresa: Yeah.

Molly: Picture the word in my head.

Theresa: Why?

Molly: So I can picture the word in my head and see what makes sense.

Theresa: [repeats Molly's words and writes on the overhead] And think about what makes sense. What are the other things? What makes sense? What...

Molly: ...word fits and sounds like language.

Theresa: [rereads from the overhead] Next time I will try to picture the word in my head and think about what makes sense, what fits and sounds like language.

Theresa used the scaffolding process to help Molly and her classmates to understand that Molly appeared to be using the syntactic cueing system when she made her initial miscue: *Miss Locket made sure*. At the same time, Theresa modeled written language on the overhead with the class to demonstrate the process of taking oral responses and constructing written meaning. Theresa paraphrased and extended the students' responses to help them draw the conclusions that Molly was proficiently using the three cueing systems simultaneously for constructing meaning. She also complimented Molly in order to continue to validate Molly's understanding of her strategy use.

Through participating in a shared reflective experience, Molly, as well as her classmates, learned metacognitive strategies for constructing meaning and keeping language intact. They demonstrated an awareness of using syntactic, semantic, and graphophonic cueing systems, and recognized the importance of meaning. Theresa served as the mediator. She facilitated Molly's reflective development and metacognitive awareness by scaffolding and assisting her reflective thinking. She probed and pushed the child's thinking through language. This verbal interaction supported the child and helped her clarify and push her thinking to a deeper level, while becoming more explicit in identifying her learning strategies.

Conclusion

Steve and Molly learned the process of reflection by interacting with Theresa and their classmates. It was only through this shared experience that each child internalized and used this mental thinking process independently. In this classroom, Theresa provided the children with many opportunities to see and practice self-reflective language, which directly influenced their potential development for higher level thinking. Through this verbal and social interaction, the children were actively constructing an understanding of their own thoughts and learning. Theresa, through this questioning, guided the students and pushed them to a more sophisticated reflection. She gently led the children, but it was the children who constructed their own meaning.

Theresa's scaffolding was akin to active listening—repeating, paraphrasing, and clarifying in a nonthreatening manner—which enabled her to clarify, elaborate, and expand the children's thinking. There were additional layers added in these demonstrations, such as repeating what the children said and then writing it down. Through this repetition, Theresa ensured that the students understood what they said, allowing them time to clarify, make the strategies more explicit, or change what they said.

By writing down what the children stated, and then rereading their thinking, Theresa could work with the children to revisit and reflect on the writing while discovering gaps in the children's thinking processes.

Through this revisiting and rereading with the teacher, the class was able to come to a deeper understanding of their thoughts. This shared activity clarified and elaborated their reflective thinking and understanding both orally and in writing. By questioning, probing, prompting, leading, repeating, rephrasing, paraphrasing, modeling, and guiding performance, Theresa was able to discover how the children constructed understanding.

Chapter 5

A Complete
Student Profile

IT IS JUNE in Theresa's second-grade classroom. Theresa
and Madeline work together at the overhead. Theresa shows
samples of Madeline's reflections in September, March, and
early June. She shares with Madeline some of the many ways in
which she has seen her reflections improve. The other students
interject positive comments about what they notice in
Madeline's reflections. Madeline comments on her own
progress and growth as a reader and writer.

inally, in the third year of our research, diagnostic instruments
began to reflect a shift in the actual strategies the reader was
using. Up to that time, some children had merely parroted
the strategies Theresa emphasized; their reflections did not match their
actual practice. Now this was changing. At this same time, the students'
reflective statements also revealed a truer picture of their metacognitive
awareness. Once the children were able to report which strategies they
were using, their reflections became richer and more detailed, and they
simultaneously demonstrated significant gains in proficiency. The community building, scaffolding, and modeling were clearly working to
help students move beyond their zone of proximal development (see
Vygotsky, 1986).

This chapter illustrates the complete reader-writer profile of Madeline, one of the second graders who participated in the fifth year of our study. Excerpts from Madeline's literacy portfolio demonstrate her significant growth as a reader-writer as well as a strong shift in her ability to reflect on a specific strategy she used to become more proficient. Madeline's ability to reflect on her own learning processes directly impacted her success as a learner. As we detail the progress we saw in Madeline, we also illustrate our own journey of discovery in coming to understand the correlation between the use of diagnostic-reflective portfolios as classroom assessment and the ways these tools support learners to become more strategic, proficient readers and writers.

Madeline's Profile

Madeline came to second grade as an emergent reader. She was extremely shy and unwilling to take any risks. Madeline believed that all questions had only one correct answer. If she did not have the "correct" answer, she would not risk a response. During reading, she relied on only one cueing system, the graphophonic. (See Madeline's reading interviews, pp. 22–24.) In her September interview, she indicated that she did not see reading as a meaning-making process; she only mentioned the graphophonic cueing system. She mentioned "blanking" almost as an afterthought to make the teacher happy. Theresa's early learning profile (p. 34) also reflected Madeline's focus on the graphophonic system. It included Theresa's plan to implement other strategies immediately. Madeline's reflections over the course of an entire year reveal her progress in reflection and assessment.

Running Records

An analysis of Madeline's running records demonstrates the shift in her strategy use and her zone of proximal development. Her first and last running records are shown for comparison (see Figures 4 and 5).

In her running record of September, Madeline's miscues were highly graphic, and there were no self-corrections or rerunnings. Her over-reliance on the graphophonic cueing system was demonstrated by seven miscues—*was/us, telling/tonight, plus/please, start/stir, pot/pan, dinner/delicious, sticky/scruffy*—only two of which were meaningful.

FIGURE 4
Madeline's September Running Record

Madeline   9/24   Stage 3 Rigby Early Emergent

Pancakes For Supper

P3 ✓✓✓✓✓
✓ day/[m] said[m]   was[c]   telling[c] ✓✓
  babysit   us   tonight

P4 ✓✓✓✓ plus[c]
  ✓✓✓ –/[sc] please

P5 ✓✓✓✓✓✓✓

P6 ✓✓✓
  ✓✓✓✓

P7 ✓✓✓✓✓   Comments

P8 ✓✓✓✓✓   Some miscues
  ✓✓✓   are meaningful.
                       Most are highly
P9 ✓✓✓ ✓✓✓✓   graphic and there
                       is little self
P10 start ✓✓   correction and no
   stir   rerunning. Melissa
   ✓✓✓   seems to be gaining
                       more confident but
P11 ✓✓✓✓   is over relying on
                       graphophonic cueing
P12 ✓✓✓✓ pot[n]   which interrupts
        pan   meaning construction.

P13 ✓✓✓✓✓
   ✓

P14 ✓✓✓✓

P15 ✓ what /✓✓✓/ dinner
      ✓   delicious

P16 so[m] sticky[m]
   oh   scruffy

All others seemed to represent the beginning sound with a guess that was not meaningful.

In November, Madeline was still using the graphophonic cueing system, but she began to use the semantic and syntactic cueing systems as well, as evidenced by seven corrections and rerunnings. She used the pictures to help her when she was unsure of words. Theresa

FIGURE 5
Madeline's May Running Record

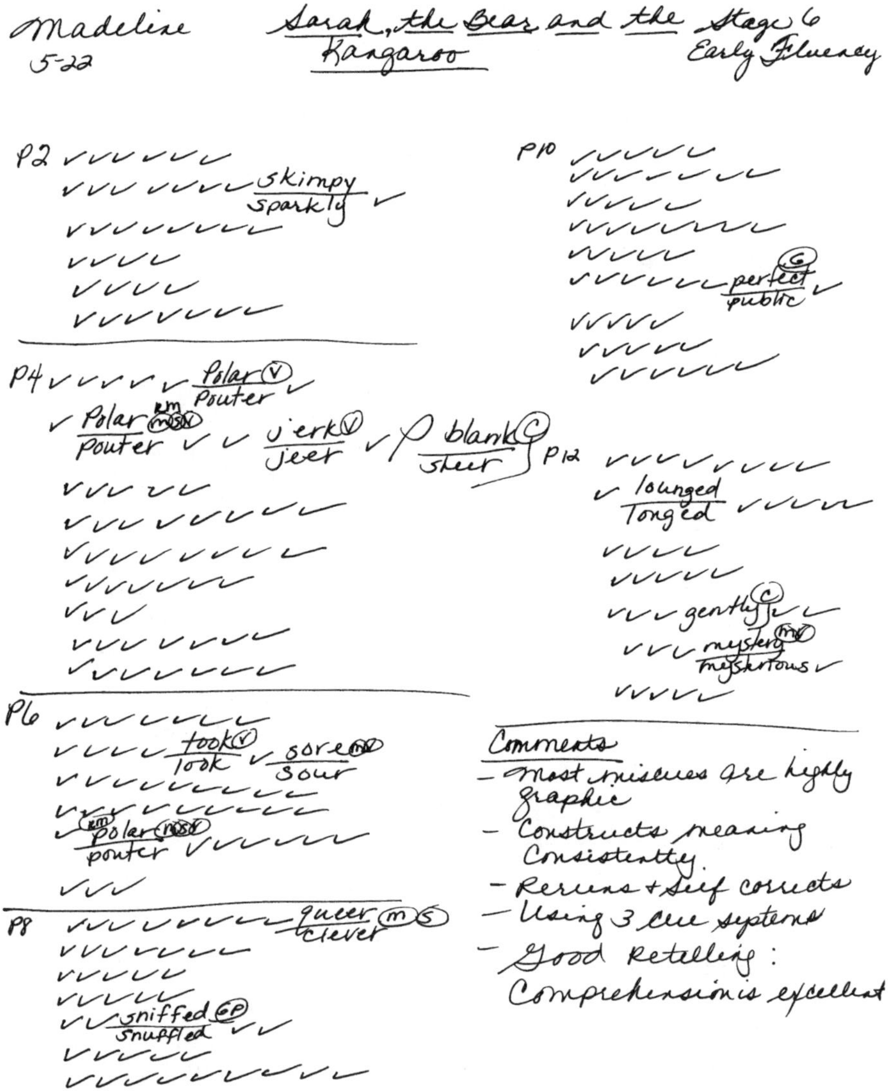

reported that Madeline's confidence was growing, as shown by both her willingness to read aloud to other students and her continued growth in making meaningful substitutions.

By February, Madeline was not only using picture clues, but she also self-corrected and reran when meaning was interrupted. Theresa encouraged her to use her blanking strategy more frequently. Still, Madeline's first response was to sound out the word.

Her running records in March and May indicated that she was using the three cueing systems and that her retellings were excellent—meaning-making had become a priority. She used the blanking strategy, reran, and self-corrected continuously. Many of her miscues were semantically and syntactically accurate.

Book Log Reflections

Madeline's reflective statements, coupled with her running records, demonstrated her shifting zone of more independent use of strategies. In Madeline's November Book Log Reflection (Figure 6), she reported that *Henry and Mudge and the Forever Sea* by Cynthia Rylant was the most difficult book she had read. She indicated that she had to say "blank" to help herself read it. To become a better reader, Madeline planned to "sauy black mor and sond out badr [say blank more and sound out better]." Her running record of the same time indicated that she was still relying strongly on the graphophonic cueing system.

By March, Madeline reported that *Henry and Mudge and the Forever Sea* was the best book because "I like the oshin [ocean]." The book that she struggled with in November had become the book that she liked best in March. *Henry and Mudge* was a beginning chapter book, and Madeline was encouraged that she was able to read it. Her enjoyment may have been deepened by her sense of accomplishment. In March, she reported the most difficult book to be *Horrible Harry in Room 2B*. She further stated that to help herself read it, "I had to say black [blank] a lot." To become a better reader, Madeline planned to "keep reeding and reed hordr [harder] books." Her running record in March corroborated her more consistent use of the blanking strategy.

By May, Madeline was still reporting *Horrible Harry in Room 2B* as the "hardest book" (see Figure 7). To help herself read it she "want back and I sad Black and I sondad [went back and I said blank and I sounded] out a little bit." In both March and May, she related that *Horrible Harry* taught her the most because it had many difficult vocabulary words. Madeline recognized the difficulty she had in reading this book, which was above

FIGURE 6
Madeline's November Book Log Reflection

1. What book did you like best? Why? JUSt A mess because it tot me to ceep my Room StRatad.

What was the easiest book to read? Why? TA Night because it olee hao a little Bφt of wos,

What was the hardest book? What did you do to help yourself read it?

HENRY anD MUDGE anD The Forever Sea Sauy Black.

What book do you remember the most? Why? in a Dark Dark Room because it has skaree stoores ano I Love skaree Starees.

What book taught you the most? How?

because uan I rad it I haUR lat my Just a mess Room be a ogan.

What are the things you want to do to become a better reader?

Sauy Black moR anD SonD Out Babr.

FIGURE 7
Madeline's May Book Log Reflection

1. What book did you like best? Why? did you

hear Someing is the book I like the best because it was scarey and I love scarey books and it just cap and getting more and more excting.

What was the easiest book to read? Why?

the snow Because it did not have a lot of words and had a lot of pachers,

What was the hardest book? What did you do to help yourself read it?

Horrible Herry in room 2B was the hardest Book. Want back and I sad Black and a little bit I sondad out,

What book do you remember the most? Why?

Arthar's valentine because I lik Valentins and sometimes wan I think of valentine I think of Arthur's valentine

What book taught you the most? How?

Horrible Herry in room 2B, It had a real lot of hard words.

What are the things you want to do to become a better reader?

I will keeping saying blank.

her level. By May, she noted that she would not only go back to the difficult word and say "blank," but that to become a better reader she would keep "saying blank." In addition, in May, Madeline had added slightly more detail to her responses. It was apparent to Madeline and to anyone who read her portfolio that the blanking strategy afforded her considerable success.

Writing Reflections

Madeline's improvement in reading paralleled a similar development in writing. A significant growth in her ability to reflect deeply and accurately about her writing revealed itself throughout the year when Theresa's class completed periodic writing reflections. (See Primary Writing Reflection in the Appendix.) Madeline chose to do her November Primary Writing Reflection (Figure 8) on her poem "The Turkeys":

The Turkeys

Turkeys have feathers,
 their color is brown
  they say gobble gobble
   and peck at the ground.
They have three toes at the end of their feet.
 They wander around to find things to eat.
  At Thanksgiving time the smart turkeys hide
   because they want to stay alive!

On the reflection, Madeline stated that she chose this piece of writing because "I really liked it" and "I really worked hard and it rims [rhymes]." When she was done, she "went back to make sure it made sence [sense]," so that when she read it, she would "understand it better." Nowhere did Madeline discuss the strategies she used to write her poem: She had painstakingly made a list of rhyming words, conferenced with different partners to see what sounded right and made sense, and revised this piece of writing several times. Madeline did realize that she worked hard to write "The Turkeys," but she could not identify what she had done to be successful.

Madeline's May Primary Writing Reflection (Figure 9) showed much more depth. She had chosen to reflect on her short story "The Puppies":

FIGURE 8
Madeline's November Primary Writing Reflection

Title _____ The turkeys

I chose this piece of writing because... I really
liked it Because I really Worked
hard and it rims

I remember when I was working on it I felt... really
realacksed.

When I was done I ... went back to make
sure it made sence.

Now when I read it, I ... understand it
better.

The things I did to help me write this were ...
think about thanksgiving.

The thing that I want to work on with other writing pieces are ...
Spelling.

FIGURE 9
Madeline's May Primary Writing Reflection

Title ___The puppies___

I chose this piece of writing because... it Shows
how I improved a little on Spellin
and on making sense when
I write.

I remember when I was working on it I for... thought
about what I could write in places
I was stuck like I put seven
puppies in and then I had a hard
time thinking of names. So I used names
of people I know.

When I was done I ...
Corrected words
made sure it made sense check
for capitols wrote periods and
final draft.

Now when I read it, It...
makes more sense because someti,
when your writing it seems like it
doesn't make sense until you go back
and read
it again

The things I did to help me write this were ...
to think about what could
happen. I also used periods to
help my story make sense.

The thing that I want to work on with other writing pieces are ...
Spelling more words correctly and
making sense every time I writ.

The Puppies

Once upon a time a little girl bought a dog. The dog was a girl. One day she had puppies she had 7 puppies. she name them Patch, Spot, Jewle, Lucky, Princess, Melissa and Mag. The puppies went for a walk in the park. The puppies met a man colled Paul. The puppies and the puppies mom liked the man The puppies and mom want with Paul they ran away to live wath Paul. and they lived happily ever after The end

This was not a story to which Madeline had devoted a great deal of time, and she was heavily influenced by the movie *101 Dalmatians*. Ironically, Madeline did not choose it because of her hard work in writing, but because of the strategies she employed to write the piece. When she was working on it, she "thought about what I could write in places I was stuck like I put seven puppies in and then I had a hard time thinking of names. So I used names of people I know." When finished, she corrected words, made sure it made sense, checked for capitals and periods, and wrote a final draft. She expressed her awareness that a writer continually needs to reread when writing because the train of thought can be lost when focusing on one word or aspect at a time.

Madeline's May reflection demonstrated a realization that she must think of her plot line during writing, and that the use of punctuation provided the reader with stopping places. This, in turn, added meaning to the story. The things she wanted to work on with other writing pieces were "spelling more words correctly and making sense every time I writ [write]." Clearly, a key point to Madeline was for the reader to understand her message. By this time, Madeline had more practice in reflecting, and her primary writing reflection was much more detailed with the "hows" of creating her story.

Goal Reflections

Madeline's goal reflections also confirmed her shift in strategy use. (See Goal Reflecting Sheet in the Appendix.) Her fall goals were,

1. Get better at reading by reading on when I get stuck on a word then going back and making sense.
2. Improve writing by spelling more words correctly.
3. Practice spelling words.

In November when Madeline reflected on her goals, she responded to "How I have been achieving my goals" by writing, "I read at school or home a lot even on the weekend to help my reading. Soding the wos [sounding the words] out and poding uot I heer [putting what I hear] in my spelling and loking [looking] in the dictionary." She still wanted to improve on her spelling and reading harder books and, "I uot to improve in macking senc [want to improve in making sense]." Again, this response demonstrated her reliance on the graphophonic cueing system and not on constructing meaning. This was corroborated by her other reflection statements in November.

Theresa and Madeline worked together to construct Madeline's second-term goals:

1. Pay more attention to the speaker by not talking when someone else is talking.
2. Practice saying "blank" and going back to reread the whole sentence.
3. Get better at spelling by using the dictionary and using other books around the room.

It was interesting to see Madeline's first goal of paying attention and not getting into trouble by talking. Madeline, who came to this class very shy, had become a social butterfly who confidently interacted with her peers. This highlighted the changes possible in a child who is immersed in a safe environment in which risk taking and questioning is acceptable and encouraged.

In March, Madeline reflected on how she had been achieving these goals: "I been staying on task and lasoning to the spakr [listening to the speaker] better and better avry [every] day and I been practiceing saying blank a lot more. I been looking in the dictionary and arond the room instead of oues [always] asking peppel [people]." She not only realized that she had changed, but was able to communicate exactly what she had done to accomplish that change. This reflection demonstrated the shifting of her zone from occasionally using the blanking strategy to more consistently constructing meaning during the reading process. Madeline extended this reflection by setting a new goal of improving on her spelling.

In May, Madeline did a final goal reflection. She reported, "I've been achieving my goal on spelling by looking in the dictionary and looking all around the room and saying the word and puting all the latters [letters] I hear. I also try to picher [picture] the words in my mend [mind]." Madeline had developed many strategies to become a better speller. She ended by stating her future goals: "I still want to improve on reading more harder books and keep saying blank. Writing more stories." This reflection demonstrated Madeline's awareness of herself as a reader who constructed meaning ("saying blank"), and as a writer whose message needed to be understood ("putting all the latters I hear" and "try to picher the words in my mend").

Oral Reading Reflections

One of the reflective pieces Theresa had children complete was a self-reflective running record. Children read a "just right" story into a tape recorder. When finished, they listened to the tape, placing one finger under the line of print to follow along as they listened. When finished, they filled out an Oral Reading Reflection. (See Oral Reading Reflection in the Appendix.)

In November, after Madeline read *Henry and Mudge and the Careful Cousin*, she reported on her Oral Reading Reflection (Figure 10) that while she was reading she had to think about what made sense and that when she came to a word she did not know, she sounded it out. Next time, she would "sau blak and sond out to [say blank and sound out too]." This response demonstrated her continual overuse of the graphophonic cueing system, which was corroborated in the running record (see p. 58), the learning profile (see p. 34), and her reading interview (see p. 22). At the time, classroom instruction was focused on making sense as a strategy, and Madeline noted it in her response. She set greater use of the blanking strategy as her goal.

By March, Madeline was reading *The Robber Pig and the Ginger Beer*. She volunteered to model the self-reflective running record for the class. Theresa had a copy of the story on the overhead and coded the running record on the overhead as the children listened to Madeline read on the tape recorder. Madeline sat at a chair at the overhead and watched Theresa code her reading. The rest of the children sat on the rug. This risk taking was a great advancement for Madeline, who in

FIGURE 10
Madeline's November Oral Reading Reflection

Name _____Madeline_____ Date _November 21_

Title _HENRY AND MUDGE AND The careful cousin_

While I was reading, I _had to thac uot uot_

mad sas _____

_____

_____ .

When I came to a word I didn't know. _____

I sonp it out _____

_____ .

When I used this strategy, it _hapt me a lattle_

_____

_____

_____ .

Next time I will _Sau Blak anp sonp oiut to_

_____

_____ .

This book was too hard, too easy, or just right. (Circle one choice.)

_____

September would not have participated and modeled for the class at all. Here is a transcript of the session:

Theresa: When you said "daf" here [pointing to the word *deaf*], what did you think you were doing?

[No response from Madeline]

What strategy were you using?

[No response]

What else do you sometimes use?

Madeline: Think of something that could make sense?

Theresa: Is *daf* a word that you know?

Madeline: No.

Theresa: Did you look at the words around it? What information that was right here did you use to help yourself?

[No response]

Anybody else think they know? Who can help her?

Molly: She was sounding out.

Theresa: Yes, I think so, too. Did it make sense?

Madeline: Not really.

Theresa: Okay, so that strategy right here did not help you make sense, but it might somewhere else. What strategy did you use first when you said "broke" for *burned*?

Madeline: Sounding out.

Theresa: Okay, then what information did you use? What were you doing here?

Madeline: Probably trying to make sense.

[Theresa points at the overhead and the miscue in question.]

Theresa: Where you went back and corrected?

Madeline: *Broke* is one word and *burned* is another.

Theresa: So you corrected it when you were trying to make sense?

Madeline:	Yes.
Theresa:	So at first you sounded out. So, the first thing you did is sound out and then you read on and you corrected it because it didn't make sense the first time. Was that a good strategy?
Class:	Yes.
Theresa:	Absolutely! Going back and correcting—reading over—is an excellent strategy that is just what good readers do.
	[Theresa reads as Madeline read the sentence.] "Mrs. Locked made some baskets."
	This word is *Lockett*; you said "Locked." Tell me about what information you used. What do you think you were doing here when you said "Locked"?
Madeline:	Probably like sounding out a little and...
Theresa:	And what? Did you know that this was a name?
Madeline:	Yes.
Theresa:	So what did you know you should do?
Madeline:	Put in a word that was probably close.
Theresa:	And do what?
Madeline:	And just go on.
Theresa:	Yes. "Mrs. Lockett made some baskets/biscuits and put them out to cool." You went back and said "biscuits." What were you doing here?
Madeline:	Sounding out.
	[Theresa points to the word *baskets* on the overhead.]
Theresa:	That was the first thing, and then what did you do?
Madeline:	I went back and said that wouldn't make sense.
Theresa:	Did you read on?
Madeline:	Yes.
Theresa:	Then you reread it and corrected it to make sense?
Madeline:	Yes.

Theresa:	"Along came the robber pig grabbing/grunting to himself." What information did you think you were using here?
	[No response]
Theresa:	This is a hard one, so I am going to help you. You were sounding out a little. The beginning and the ending sounds are the same. But listen to this: "Along came the robber pig, grabbing." Could that make sense so far?
Madeline:	Yes.
Class:	No.
Theresa:	Can *grabbing* make sense in this sentence if we don't look at the words on the page?
Class:	No.
Theresa:	Why doesn't that make sense? It could have been, "Along came the robber pig, grabbing everything he could." Does that sound like language so far? Up to the miscue?
Class:	Yes.
Al:	But when you read on...
Theresa:	But when you read on you realize that it doesn't make sense. It still sounds like language, but it doesn't make sense. Right here [pointing to previous miscue: *baskets/biscuits*] Madeline was making sense and she was sounding like language and she was also trying to put in a word that fit. Did she go back [pointing to the current miscue] and correct after she went on here?
Madeline:	No.
Class:	No.
Theresa:	No, she didn't correct. So sometimes you were correcting and sometimes you were reading on. So you have your strategies down that you need to make sense. You just need to make sure that you are using

	them all of the time. Do you see what you need to be looking for when you are listening to your own tapes?
Class:	Yes.
Theresa:	Any questions about this so far?
Class:	No.
Theresa:	While I was reading I _____ when I came to a word I didn't know.
Madeline:	I sounded out.
Theresa:	What else did you do?
Madeline:	And went back.
Theresa:	And?
Madeline:	And corrected, too.
Theresa:	Well, why did you correct?
Madeline:	To make sense.

[Theresa writes on overhead, *Sounded out and went back and corrected to make sense.*]

Theresa:	When I used this strategy it...
	[No response]
	What did it do for you while you were reading?
Madeline:	Sometimes it worked and sometimes it didn't.
Theresa:	Why do you think sometimes it didn't?
Madeline:	Some words don't sound like, they don't sound like they're spelled. They sound different. Sounding out doesn't always work.
Theresa:	Is that why you always need to go back and correct? When you go back you are always trying to make sense and sound like language.
Madeline:	Okay.
Theresa:	Can I also go back and add what you just told me?
Madeline:	Yes.
Theresa:	It helped me to say "blank" and go back and then read it over and put in a word that makes sense and

	sounds like language. It helped to go back and make sense, is that the second part of it?
Madeline:	Yes.
Theresa:	You said, "Sometimes it worked and sometimes it didn't." That's the sounding out part. But you went back and corrected, so you were thinking about the sounds, but you also had to see what made sense and sounded like language?
Madeline:	When I read it, I go back and think just how someone would say it.
Theresa:	Madeline just told us that when she goes back she thinks about how someone would say it.
	[To "sometimes it worked and sometimes it didn't," Theresa now adds, "It helped to go back and make sense and sound like language."]
	What did you always do before?
Madeline:	Sound out.
Theresa:	Do you go back and check to see if it makes sense all of the time?
Madeline:	No.
Class:	No.
Theresa:	What are you going to do next time?
	[No response]
	When you are reading, to help yourself, what strategies are you going to keep doing or add?
Madeline:	Say "blank."
Theresa:	And do what?
Madeline:	Go back.
Theresa:	And then do what?
Madeline:	Read it over.
Theresa:	And do what?
Madeline:	Put in a word that makes sense.
Theresa:	And?

Madeline:	And sounds like language.
Theresa:	Madeline, I think that what I hear you saying here is that next time, instead of trying to sound out first, that you are going to make sense first and then go back and make sure it will fit by looking at the sounds and making sure it makes sense. So, you are actually going to check that it makes sense and then check the sounds and the language.
	[Madeline nods her head "yes" and smiles.]
	Does that sound like a good strategy?
Madeline:	Yes.
Class:	Yes.
Theresa:	Do you think that this will help Madeline get even better as a reader?
Madeline:	Yes.
Class:	Yes.
Theresa:	Madeline, have you come a long way?
Madeline:	[with a big smile] Yes.
Theresa:	What did you used to always do?
Madeline:	Sound out.
Theresa:	Did you always go back and correct it when it didn't make sense?
Madeline:	No.
Theresa:	So you have made a lot of progress.

When Theresa first questioned what strategy Madeline was using, after initially making no response, Madeline stated the strategy of making sense because she knew that was the response Theresa would like her to make. Theresa further probed Madeline, but Madeline was unable to voice the strategy and was confused here. Theresa used the scaffolding process to assist Madeline and the class in understanding that Madeline relied on only the graphophonic cueing system when she said "daf," a nonsense word for the text word *deaf*. Theresa then pointed to *broke* for the text word *burned*. Madeline read "broke" instead of *burned*, and then read to the end of the sentence and corrected the miscue that did not make sense. Theresa continued to scaffold in order to help Madeline become metacognitively aware that she focused on making sense in that particular miscue. Theresa pointed out the importance of correcting a miscue that does not make sense. Theresa praised Madeline for using a strategy that all good readers would use.

Theresa then focused Madeline's attention to the miscue *baskets* for *biscuits*. Madeline had self-corrected. Through questioning, Theresa helped Madeline state that she corrected because putting baskets out to cool did not make sense. Theresa probed and questioned in order to clarify Madeline's thinking. Madeline's responses to the questions became faster, and she eventually demonstrated that she was more sure of her responses. Her initial confusion at the beginning was clarified. Theresa pointed out that *grabbing/grunting* was a miscue that was different from the previous miscues. Through probing, Theresa demonstrated that it read like language up to the point of the miscue. However, with Al's help, Theresa pointed out that after the miscue, the sentence stopped making sense.

Theresa also pointed out that sometimes Madeline corrected her miscues and sometimes she did not. Theresa's intent was to bring to Madeline's awareness the need to apply her meaning-constructing strategies consistently. Theresa wrote on the overhead *Sounded out and went back and corrected to make sense.* Again, Theresa prompted to bring the strategy to Madeline's awareness and to help Madeline assess her use of strategies fully. Theresa moved on to the next prompt on the Oral Reading Reflection sheet.

Theresa scaffolded with questioning and rephrasing to help Madeline realize that using all three cueing systems (semantic, syntactic, and graphophonic) was a high-level strategy. Madeline was actually able to extend her thinking to incorporate the syntactic cueing system when she stated, "I go back and think just how someone would say it." Theresa wrote on the overhead as they scaffolded together. She reread the final entry for the class. Theresa continually prodded with simple extensions "And do what?" or "And?" to draw out the complete strategy. The plan for future action with Madeline focused on making sense, particularly making sure the word fits and makes sense. Theresa paraphrased and clarified Madeline's words to ensure that

Madeline was aware that this was the first strategy she needed to consistently apply in her reading.

Theresa prodded and probed to help Madeline and the class realize that they needed to use the three cueing systems in meaning construction during the reading process. Theresa further praised Madeline to continue to validate Madeline's understanding of her strategy use.

Through scaffolding, Theresa made Madeline aware of the strategies she used when reading. Theresa's interactions with Madeline pushed the frontier of Madeline's own thinking and understanding of herself as a learner. Through diagnosis, past observations, and listening to Madeline, Theresa recognized that Madeline's zone had shifted. Therefore, she prompted and probed as Madeline reflected in order to help her understand and control her own learning. Braun (1993) states that the zone of proximal development "stretches the limits of [the teacher's] potential to create the expert assistance that both defines the zones and assists the learner in moving from his actual development level to his potential level" (p. 86). Theresa served as the expert to scaffold Madeline's understanding of reading strategies. Through this process, Madeline was eventually able to set a goal to "say 'blank'...go back...read it over...put in a word that makes sense...and sounds like language." This cooperative reflection episode was a real breakthrough for Madeline, and she began to use the blanking strategy consistently in her reading instead of always relying on graphophonics first. This was a turning point for Madeline as a reader, as well as for other members of the class.

In June, Madeline worked individually on a reflection about her oral reading of *Harry Hates Shopping* (see Figure 11). She had shifted to thinking about what makes sense and sounds like language as a strategy when she came to a word she did not know. She set a goal to continue using this strategy and others. This reflection showed that Madeline had become aware of her reading strategies and knew what she must continue to do in order to construct meaning.

Madeline's running records, reading interview, and portfolio reflections worked together with Theresa's observations to help Theresa expand her understanding of Madeline as a reader and writer.

FIGURE 11
Madeline's June Oral Reading Reflection

Name _____ *Madeline* _____ Date ___ 6·2 ___

Title ___ Harry **hates** shopping _____

While I was reading, I _*thought* *what* *could*_

*make sans and sound like language*

_____

_____ .

When I came to a word I didn't know. _____

_____

_____ .

When I used this strategy, it ___ *halped me figure*

*the word out.*

_____

_____ .

Next time I will __ *keep useing the same*

*strategy and other ones*

_____ .

This book was too hard, too easy, or just right. (Circle one choice.)

_____

Other Reflection Forms

Theresa used several additional reflection forms in the diagnostic-reflective portfolios. (See Reading Response Reflection, Word Bank Reflection, What My Portfolio Shows About Me, and Comments in the Appendix.) The children completed reading responses and for their portfolios selected the reading response that demonstrated their growth as a responder to literature. The Reading Response Reflection guided them through written reflections. The Word Bank Reflection was used during the portfolio reflection period to make the children more conscious of their growth and development and of the vast number of words they were learning. Theresa used What My Portfolio Shows About Me to lead children to a more reflective stance at the conclusion of their portfolio construction. The form brought children through a summary of their portfolio and prompted children to establish new goals for the beginning of the new marking period. Theresa used the Comments form to synthesize her collective understanding of the child as a literacy learner. Parents also were invited to write to the child on this form. All of these forms contributed to developing a more reflective stance in the children.

Conclusion

Throughout this assessment process, students were engaged in inquiry. They were expected to question their own learning, the texts they read, and the processes they actively used to construct meaning. The students' reflections demonstrated their growth as readers and their attainment of a deeper, more meaningful understanding of the learning process regardless of their level of proficiency. In addition, as students recognized the difference between the strategies they thought they used and the process they actually followed, they were able to make adjustments to gain control of the reading process.

Over time, students were able to reflect on and evaluate their own work. Through scaffolding, practice, and use, the children became better at reflection and increased their awareness of "what they [had] learned (content), how they [had] learned (process), and why they [had] learned (purpose)" (Short, Harste, & Burke, 1996, p. 362). Through the continual process of discussing what they knew and how they knew it, the children made discoveries about their learning. As they understood more about their own processes as readers and writers, they became better at both. Through the process of reflection, they monitored their own learning, began to understand themselves better as learners, and became more capable of establishing meaningful goals for themselves and their future learning.

These children practiced the process of reflection and became comfortable with it. Theresa scaffolded the language for them, and they made it their own. Through scaffolding, the children listened and learned in new ways. What was once their assisted level of reflection became their independent level.

Through her constant observations of the children's zones, Theresa learned more about them. As a result, she was better able to prompt and probe their thinking. She became an expert at knowing how to get them to look at their own learning. Braun (1993) states that "as the child learns to monitor his learning with the prompting and probing of the teacher, he becomes more reflective and increasingly in control of his learning. Part of that control involves knowing when to ask for assistance and knowing what kind of assistance he needs—a problem-solving approach to helping himself" (p. 85). The children and Theresa collected the data and interpreted it. Theresa made each child's learning visible, and each child became more capable of monitoring his or her own learning. Their reflections were evidence of their growth as readers, writers, and thinkers, and enabled them to make discoveries about their literacy development.

The success of our diagnostic-reflective portfolios was a tribute to the collaborative spirit involved in constructing them. Both the teacher and the students had vested interests in the portfolios, and each was equally proud of what was contributed to the construction. The teacher contributed the diagnosis and the scaffolding that helped lead the children to a higher level of independence and awareness of their learning. The children had evidence of their progress as learners. The portfolios became public documents that demonstrated each student's growth over time: a powerful statement to the student, teacher, parents, administrators, friends, and relatives.

The process of selection and reflection on the contents of the portfolio enabled each child to see new possibilities as a learner. The child's portfolio and reflections directed the teacher to new possibilities for instruction. Each portfolio construction and reflection point was a stimulus for the child and teacher to collaborate together in order to plan goals for the future. Through this process, the portfolio served as a vehicle to refine and guide learning and instruction. The portfolio was a tool that supported the child's own reflection and learning. Rief (1992) puts it well:

> The act of putting together a portfolio is a reflective act in itself, as students choose what to put in there and why. That reflection on where they've been, where they are now, and how they got there is what real learning is all about. (p. 145)

Chapter 6

Conclusion

eporting students' strengths, needs, and overall literacy development has been an ongoing struggle for conscientious educators. During our journey of discovery, we have explored diagnostic-reflective portfolios as a way to help ourselves and the students experience new avenues to demonstrate components of literacy development. We have come to a new understanding of portfolio construction and reflection. Our journey continually leads us to question further and enables us to see literacy from a broader perspective. It allows us to define reading and writing as ongoing processes from which learners construct meaning. Our experiences suggest that participating in the construction of developing diagnostic-reflective portfolios positively influences the literacy development of students.

Our concepts of developing a classroom culture, our understanding of the language cueing systems, and our analysis of miscues guide our discussions, discoveries, and practices in working with children we teach. The work of Vygotsky (1978, 1986) also motivates Theresa to empower the readers and writers with a deeper understanding of the process of their own learning through scaffolded reflection in the zone of proximal development.

Theresa models oral reflection, making her thought processes accessible to the students. In the process, the metacognitive line is built and strengthened in each learner because Theresa elicits and mediates the children's understanding through a scaffolded oral reflection. The learning process is explained, clarified, and extended for each child. In turn, the children are able to verbalize their use of reading strategies and are empowered with a conscious awareness of their learning. According to Di Bello and Orlich (1987), the process of verbalizing one's current method of knowing makes the understanding explicit. Our study not only supports this premise, but allows for the internalization of these learned strategies. Theresa continually asks children to reflect on their own learning with partners, with the teacher, as a model, and by themselves in order for them to gain a deeper understanding of their own learning processes. Porter and Cleland (1995) state, "The portfolio helps to bring what we have learned about learning to a conscious level" (pp. 137–138).

The belief system that we share as educators and practitioners influenced the readers and writers in this second-grade classroom. As colleagues, we constantly challenge, mediate, and influence each other's respective thinking. We acknowledge that literacy is as much a social process as it is a linguistic process. We value and respect the language learning that exists for children long before they enter the classroom, and we use this knowledge to build strong, literate learners.

Theresa facilitates the learning in the classroom through the explicit discussions she conducts with the children to help "demythify and demystify" their understanding of the reading process itself (Goodman & Marek, 1996, p. 203). This continuous talking, thinking, learning, and wondering about language, reading, and writing are guided by her own belief systems, which in turn directly affect what her students believe about their own reading. The discussions concerning the cueing systems used in the reading process, the highlighting of what good readers and writers do, and the sharing of wonderful literature all set the tone for the way readers and writers see themselves. The whole classroom atmosphere is built on community: a safe place where children are made aware of their reading and writing processes through discussions, teacher diagnosis, teacher and student demonstration, goal setting, questioning, inquiry, reflection, scaffolding, and creating portfolios.

This environment of caring and risk taking transforms second graders into readers and writers who take responsibility for their own learning. All of the students come to value and respect themselves as literacy learners and as members of a literate community. Goodman and Marek (1996) point out, "When readers are in environments that encourage risk-taking with teachers who respect them as knowledgeable about their own reading, they begin to depend on themselves as the most important resource to answer their questions as they read" (p. 205).

The teacher's diagnosis, students' demonstration, and reflection by both inform Theresa's awareness of each child's literacy development, which enables her to make informed instructional decisions to move each child forward in the literacy process. Diagnosis should be a "point where learning is initiated rather than concluded" (Porter & Cleland, 1995, p. 145). Diagnosis enables the teacher to construct appropriate goals that help children gain proficiency in reading and writing, and help them become aware of the strategies they use to become literate. Theresa recognizes where a child is making progress and supports this development and movement through the use of the diagnostic-reflective portfolio process. She matches the diagnosis with the child's demonstration, reflecting with the child to create goals for literacy improvement. The melding of diagnosis, demonstration, and goal setting influences students' reflections, leading them to more consistently and consciously implement strategies that improve reading proficiency.

Skillful kidwatching enables the teacher to recognize each child's readiness for learning and to support his or her growth and development. Goodman and Goodman (1990) state, "Teachers know how to create conditions that will cause learners to exhibit and make the most of their zones of proximal development" (p. 236). Within these zones, Theresa scaffolds the language-learning process with her students. Through demonstrations and reflections like those we have shown with Madeline, Theresa helps students create a bridge from established practices to new and developing strategies. As students become more aware of their own learning strategies, they are able to construct meaning through reading and writing rich texts. These authentic literacy experiences give both Theresa and the students many reciprocal opportunities to look closely at the social and linguistic constructions of language. In return, Theresa's students become highly competent users of language throughout all of their literacy learning.

To be successful readers and writers, students must be in classrooms that "Yetta Goodman would describe as dripping with literacy" (Harwayne, 1993, p. 323). Readers and writers must have large blocks of uninterrupted time to practice these authentic literacy experiences. In Theresa's classroom students are immersed in reading, writing, thinking, speaking, listening, wondering, questioning, and reflecting. They can choose what to read, write, and reflect on, and Theresa serves as a role model who reads, writes, and reflects.

The learning community provides a safe atmosphere in which children of all abilities work together, build on strengths, and overcome weaknesses in order for all students to experience success. Because Theresa selects a wide range of learners to model literacy-learning practice and reflection, all her students feel comfortable and worthwhile. As Goodman and Marek (1996) state,

> It is important...to include in such discussions a wide range of readers so that less confident readers come to understand the reading strategies and language cueing systems that all readers use, including those they consider to be good readers. (p. 204)

The everyday struggles that accompany all interactive teaching practices were certainly felt throughout the implementation of portfolios in Theresa's classroom. Both Theresa and the students met with points of confusion regarding the use of strategies and the establishment of goals and objectives for teaching, learning, and meaningful evaluation. Theresa strove to maintain the integrity of meaningful literacy practices, at the same time struggling to provide for shared ownership of literacy assessment and evaluation. Through these struggles, her own understanding of scaffolding within the zone of proximal development was strengthened. These very practices allowed her a deeper understanding of students' language and literacy processes and in turn caused her to reflect much more deeply on her own teaching. She came to understand that the construction of portfolios was a process that for all students would be subject to their own developmental understandings of learning. This raised consciousness for Theresa and her students and enabled them to negotiate a strong, focused, collaborative journey toward practical and meaningful learning and assessment.

Each year is a new journey of discovery. Each June, we debrief and reflect about what we have learned over the course of the year. We celebrate the growth and development of the learners in the classroom, the increased risk taking, and the growth of the inquiry process. We determine the procedures that worked well, recognize the reflection guides that elicited the deepest reflections, note those that need revisions, detail the strategies the learners have discussed, and review the reflective discussions that took place. Through this process, we come to recognize the gaps in the students' learning and reflection, as well as in our own. The process also helps us identify and discover the gaps in instruction. Reflective exploration enables us to set new goals for the forthcoming year as we continue our journey with each new set of students.

We continue on our journey of discovery. We are not only teachers, but learners. We do not pretend to have all the answers. We make new discoveries every day. The students challenge our thinking and broaden our perspective in new ways. It is only by taking small steps and risks in our journey through portfolio development that the wide range of possibilities for any portfolio implementation process become more clear. Continued questioning and reflection of the practices we implement will clarify, refine, and extend us through our own zones of proximal development.

Each year we change and grow with our portfolios. We do not offer a formula for portfolios. Rather, we offer a journey of discovery in a second-grade classroom. Like Graves (1992) we believe that you need to "keep a good idea growing," otherwise portfolios will get locked into a "rigid process" (p. 1). Portfolio possibilities are limitless; we challenge teachers to venture into their own journey of discovery.

Afterword

For us, diagnostic-reflective portfolios were not only a means of assessment, but also a catalyst for change. It was our desire to change the way that student literacy was evaluated, to involve the students in meaningful reflection of their own learning, and to make our instruction as relevant and informed as possible. It has been a long process of constructing, searching for, and clarifying our own meaning as educators:

> Assume that any significant innovation, if it is to result in change, requires individual implementers to work out their own meaning. Significant change involves a certain amount of ambiguity, ambivalence and uncertainty for the individual about the meaning of the change. Thus, effective implementation is a process of clarification. (Rhodes & Shanklin, 1993, p. 455)

Here we each share personal reflections on our journey of discovery, along with some final thoughts for you as you embark on your own journey.

Ann

I have always believed that learning is a journey. My journey in learning about diagnostic-reflective portfolios began with many bumps along the road, wrong turns, and yellow lights. The detours Theresa and I took as we looked at how assessment informs instruction and the importance of student reflection allowed for time to downshift and rethink our destination and to plan accordingly.

Our investigation of portfolios was complex and filled with uncertainty. We shared long hours of conversation over the value and purpose of portfolio assessment. There were numerous discussions about assessing learners' abilities and what the teacher should do with the respective information. There were many points of confusion, but guided by our theory, we pushed past our uncertainties and became as reflective about our teaching as we asked our students to be about their learning.

One of our most thought-provoking conversations took place as Theresa and I sat in a hotel room in a large city on the night before we were to make a national conference presentation. We spent the entire evening discussing the progress we had made and what we were seeing from some of the reflection sheets and the portfolio project itself. After a long and lively debate, we recognized that we were practicing the process we taught in Theresa's classroom. We were prompting, questioning, probing, and directing each other to elicit concrete evidence, and as a result, we were able to see things in new ways. We both came to new understandings about literacy teaching and learning that would inform further instruction in the classroom.

Our research was reshaped through this process, and with each new understanding came growth in the teaching and learning of literacy and the importance of grounded, valid assessment. It was challenging and rewarding, and it enabled us to seek new findings, which provided evidence of growth and the value of our research. We constantly acted as teachers, guides, mentors, facilitators, and learners, putting on these roles like overcoats. Sometimes we were unsure of our direction, but in much the same way as we believed the children needed to reflect, we needed a whole lot of talking to gain an awareness level of what was going on.

As teachers committed to engaging students in reflection, we considered teaching to be a lifelong learning process that we engaged in every day. Theresa and I saw teaching as more than the transmission of knowledge. There were no winners or losers in the classroom. We passionately believed that all children could learn no matter what their background was. I believed that the successful classroom teacher would be knowledgeable and reflective, and would have an enormous and enduring impact on each and every learner. As a reflective practitioner, Theresa was always in the process of reconsidering, refining, and renewing her assumptions about language, literacy, and assessment.

I want to thank Theresa, who courageously let me into her classroom and showed me all of her teaching. She opened up not only her classroom but also her heart and her life for examination and reflection. She has nourished my own practice with young learners, challenged and deepened my thinking, and brought joy to this research project. Her insights and exuberance have forever influenced me. Theresa has instilled a love of reading, writing, and literature in her students, and she has also helped them become reflective about their learning.

The process of hypothesizing, questioning, seeing, analyzing, and reflecting was at times painful, but always rewarding. I hope that the theory shines through the practice. This journey of discovery has forever changed my thinking about literacy learning and I hope it accomplishes the same thing for you. May this book set you on your own journey of discovery and help you create learning communities that transform children and their literacy development.

Theresa

As a graduate student and beginning teacher, I was desperately trying to understand theories of literacy learning and how they related to classroom practices. In frustration, I sought out the expertise of the most knowledgeable and passionate college professor I had ever encountered. After we spent many office hours discussing and debating, our research project was born. When I look back now, I understand that my frustration came with the evolution of learning as I constructed new beliefs and challenged old assumptions. The outdated reporting system at my school simply did not convey the amazing growth that both my students and I experienced as they constructed themselves as readers and writers before my eyes in what seemed like an ordinary second-grade classroom.

There is no way to express the fear or the joy that came out of those learning experiences in the first few years I spent as a classroom teacher. The blood, sweat, tears, sleeplessness, friendship, and professional development have changed my life in ways that I continue to discover every day. I am now and forever will be an advocate for teachers, for the overwhelming responsibilities we take on to educate other people's children. I have also become a passionate advocate of teacher and student reflection, progressive literacy teaching practices, high expectations for all students regardless of background, and teacher support groups. Without these, I would not be the coauthor of this book.

In each of the classrooms at my school, where teachers use portfolios, there is a familiar buzz at the end of each marking term as students and teachers work together to construct new understandings about the learning that has taken place over 3 months. Through my own journey of discovery and those of my wonderful colleagues, I have come to understand that portfolios take on a life of their own and are most reflective of the classrooms from which they come. Portfolios are as much a reflection of the values, practices, and beliefs within a classroom culture as they are of the individual growth that is demonstrated through the portfolio itself. Most important, we continue to value the learners' insights about their own progress and use this process to inform and refine our teaching practices.

I thank Ann for offering me the opportunity to become a reflective practitioner. Without her vision, devotion, friendship, support, and unrelenting commitment, I would not have had the strength to see this project through. Her support has helped me grow as a teacher of literacy both to young students and future educators, pursue my professional goals, and advocate for meaningful assessment practices during tough times in education. Her commitment to my students, to meaningful assessment, and to me has had an impact on my life that words can never describe. Our journey of discovery goes on and on as we strengthen our commitment to quality literacy teaching and meaningful assessment.

As this project comes to completion, I set my sights on the future and once again reshape my thinking about literacy, classrooms, and assessment. As I push on toward new research endeavors, my personal journey of discovery continues to evolve. The stories of Madeline, Ben, Molly, Dan, Steve, and all of the other students who have changed my life and my teaching forever will be with me as I strive for continued understanding of literacy learning and literacy assessment. It is the stories of these students that keep my commitment and dedication to these topics alive, and it is my wish that their stories in part do the same for the teachers who will get to know them in this book.

If you are reading these reflections, you have already embarked on your own journey. Most likely, you are reflecting on the practices in your classroom as you are reading this. I hope that our own uncertainties and the successes of our students will encourage you along your way.

Appendix

Reading Interview

(Adapted from the Carolyn Burke Reading Interview)

1. When you are reading and you come to something you don't know, what do you do?

    Do you ever do anything else?

2. Who is a good reader that you know?

3. What makes him/her a good reader?

4. Do you think she or he ever comes to something she or he doesn't know?

5. If "Yes"—When _____ does come to something she or he doesn't know, what do you think she or he does?

    If "No"—Suppose she or he does come to something she or he doesn't know. What do you think she or he would do?

    Do you think she or he ever does anything else?

6. If you knew someone was having trouble reading, how would you help that person?

7. What would a/your teacher do to help that person?

8. How did you learn to read?

9. What would you like to do better as a reader?

10. Do you think you are a good reader? Why?

Retelling Outline

Title:_____

Author: _____

Assign points to each section as appropriate so that the total score is out of 100.

Characters (_____ points each):

Character Development (_____ points each):

Character points total _____

Setting (_____ points each):

Setting points total _____

Events (_____ points each):

Events points total _____

Plot (_____ points each):

Plot points total _____

Theme (_____ points each):

Theme points total _____

Total Retelling Points: _____

Temporary Spelling Evaluation

Name: _____ Grade: _____

Date:	/	/	/	/
Precommunicative String of letters or symbols. e.g., mrbsopnd				
Semiphonetic One-, two-, three-letter spellings. Some letter/sound correspondence. e.g., wnt – went Dg – dog				
Phonetic Close match between sounds and letters. e.g., becos – because Wot – what Sed – said				
Transitional Less reliance on sounds. Close to standard spelling. Greater reliance on visual aspects of print. e.g., House – house				

Reading Checklist

Name: _____ Grade: _____ Date: _____

Date:	/	/	/	/
Reading Attitudes				
Enjoys books				
Chooses to read				
Self-selects appropriate books				
Shared Book Experience				
Listens attentively				
Joins in when able				
Responds to text, questions, pictures				
Reading Strategies				
Understands directionality				
Understands 1-1 matching				
Reads for meaning				
Uses semantic cues (meaning)				
Uses syntactic cues (structure, grammar)				
Uses graphophonic cues (sound/symbol)				
Uses picture cues				
Uses initial and final consonant				
Uses digraphs				
Uses consonant blends				
Uses vowels and vowel combinations				
Makes predictions				
Self-corrects errors				
Recognizes high-frequency words				
Reads fluently				
Uses print about the room				
Comprehension				
Can retell a story in own words				
Can figure out word from context				
Can analyze and think critically				
Other				

Writing Checklist

(Developed by Ludlow Public Schools, Ludlow, MA, USA)

Child's Name:_____

Circle Grade Level: Kindergarten   Grade 1   Grade 2   Grade 3

School Year: _____

	1st term	2nd term	3rd term
Fluency and Coherence			
Understands that written language conveys meaning			
Able to choose and develop own topic			
Writing makes sense			
Writing has "voice" (style)			
Process			
Uses prewriting strategies			
Able to retell/read own work			
Participates in conferences and group shares as author/audience			
Able to organize information			
Revises for content			
Edits for mechanics			
Takes pieces to publication			
Mechanics			
Writes complete sentences where appropriate			
Uses capital letters appropriately (specify)			
Uses punctuation appropriately (specify)			
Uses functional and standard spelling appropriately			
Understands when legibility and neatness are important			

	1st term	2nd term	3rd term
Attitude			
Willing to write/takes pride in writing			
Chooses to share writing with others			
Developing confidence as a writer			
Takes risks in writing			
Willing to assist others with writing			

Teacher Comments:

Parent Comments:

Evaluation Key:
    NTA Needs time and assistance
    MP   Making progress
    DC   Demonstrates consistency

Elementary Reading Attitude Survey

School_____ Grade_____ Name _____

1. How do you feel when you read a book on a rainy Saturday?

2. How do you feel when you read a book in school during free time?

3. How do you feel about reading for fun at home?

4. How do you feel about getting a book for a present?

5. How do you feel about spending free time reading?

6. How do you feel about starting a new book?

7. How do you feel about reading during summer vacation?

8. How do you feel about reading instead of playing?

9. How do you feel about going to a bookstore?

10. How do you feel about reading different kinds of books?

Reprinted from McKenna, Michael C., & Kear, Dennis J. (1990, May). Measuring attitude toward reading: A new tool for teachers. *The Reading Teacher, 43*(9), 626–639.

11. How do you feel when the teacher asks you questions about what you read?

12. How do you feel about doing reading workbook pages and worksheets?

13. How do you feel about reading in school?

14. How do you feel about reading your school books?

15. How do you feel about learning from a book?

16. How do you feel when it's time for reading class?

17. How do you feel about the stories you read in reading class?

18. How do you feel when you read out loud in class?

19. How do you feel about using a dictionary?

20. How do you feel about taking a reading test?

Routine Self-Evaluation

What new thing did I learn today?

What confused me?

What did I like?

What did I dislike?

What did I achieve today?

How did I learn today (from discussions with others, from doing activities by myself, by doing activities with others, by thinking hard, by redoing my work, by working with a partner, by questioning the teacher, etc.)?

How was my performance in class today?

Book Log Reflection

1. What book did you like best? Why?

2. What was the easiest book to read? Why?

3. What was the hardest book? What did you do to help yourself read it?

4. What book do you remember the most? Why?

5. What book taught you the most? How?

6. What are the things you want to do to become a better reader?

Primary Writing Reflection

I chose this piece of writing because…

I remember when I was working on it I felt…

When I was done I…

Now when I read it, I…

The things I did to help me write this were…

The things that I want to work on with other writing pieces are…

Goal Reflecting Sheet

How I have been achieving my goals:

_____

_____

_____

_____

_____

_____

_____

What I still want to improve:

_____

_____

_____

_____

_____

_____

_____

Oral Reading Reflection

Name _____ Date _____

Title _____

While I was reading, I _____

_____

_____

_____ .

When I came to a word I didn't know, _____

_____

_____

_____ .

When I used this strategy, it _____

_____

_____

_____ .

Next time I will _____

_____

_____

_____ .

This book was too hard, too easy, or just right. (Circle one choice.)

Reading Response Reflection

I chose to put this reading response in my portfolio because…

This piece of work shows…

I chose to respond to this book because…

If I were the author/illustrator of this book I…

Word Bank Reflection

I have learned to read more than _____ words this term.

I have learned to spell more than _____ words this term.

Some of the words I have learned to read are

_____	_____
_____	_____
_____	_____
_____	_____

Some of the new words I can spell are

_____	_____
_____	_____
_____	_____
_____	_____

The things I have done to get better at reading are

_____

_____

_____

The things I have done to get better at spelling are

_____

_____

_____

The things I can do to keep getting better are

_____

_____

_____

What My Portfolio Shows About Me

The things I have learned are…

The things I still want to improve on are…

The things I have gotten better at are…

The new goals I have are…

How I have worked to achieve my present goals…

Comments

My Teacher's Thoughts and Reflections

_____

_____

_____

_____

_____

_____

_____

_____

My Parents' Thoughts and Reflections

_____

_____

_____

_____

_____

_____

_____

_____

References

Anthony, R., Johnson, T., Mickelson, N., & Preece, A. (1991). *Evaluating literacy: A perspective for change*. Portsmouth, NH: Heinemann.

Benedict, S. (1994). Looking at their own words: Students' assessment of their own writing. In K. Holland, D. Bloome, & J. Solsken (Eds.), *Alternative perspectives in assessing children's language and literacy* (pp. 134–156). Norwood, NJ: Ablex.

Bergamini, J. (1993). An English department portfolio project. In M.A. Smith & M. Ylvisaker (Eds.), *Teachers' voices: Portfolios in the classroom* (pp. 145–159). Berkeley, CA: National Writing Project.

Bloome, D. (1994). You can't get there from here. In K. Holland, D. Bloome, & J. Solsken (Eds.), *Alternative perspectives in assessing children's language and literacy* (pp. 55–72). Norwood, NJ: Ablex.

Bodrova, E., & Leong, J. (1996). *Tools of the mind: The Vygotskian approach to early childhood education*. Englewood Cliffs, NJ: Prentice Hall.

Braun, C. (1993). *Looking, listening and learning: Observing and assessing young readers*. Winnipeg, MB: Peguis.

Brown, A. (1978). Knowing when, where, and how to remember: A problem of metacognition. In R. Glaser (Ed.), *Advances in instructional psychology*. Hillsdale, NJ: Erlbaum.

Bruner, J. (1983). *Child's talk: Learning to use language*. New York: W.W. Norton.

Cazden, C. (1988). *Classroom discourse: The language of teaching and learning*. Portsmouth, NH: Heinemann.

Clay, M. (1985). *The early detection of reading difficulties* (3rd ed.). Portsmouth, NH: Heinemann.

Cochran-Smith, M. (1984). *The making of a reader*. Norwood, NJ: Ablex.

Courtney, A.M. (1987). *Becoming literate*. Unpublished doctoral dissertation, University of Massachusetts, Amherst.

Courtney, A.M., & Abodeeb, T.L. (1999). Diagnostic-reflective portfolios. *The Reading Teacher, 52*, 708–714.

Davydov, V.V. (1986). Problems of developmental teaching: The experience of theoretical and experimental psychological research. *Soviet Education, 30*, 66–79.

Di Bello, L., & Orlich, F. (1987). How Vygotsky's notion of "scientific concept" may inform contemporary studies of theory development. *Quarterly Newsletter of the Laboratory of Comparative Human Cognition, 9*(3), 96–99.

Edelsky, C., Altwerger, B., & Flores, B. (1991). *Whole language: What's the difference?* Portsmouth, NH: Heinemann.

Gal'perin, P.Y. (1969). Stages of development of mental acts. In M. Cole & I. Maltzmann (Eds.), *A handbook of contemporary soviet psychology* (pp. 249–273). New York: Basic Books.

Genishi, C., & Dyson, A. (1984). *Language assessment in the early years*. Norwood, NJ: Ablex.

Gentry, J.R., & Gillet, J.W. (1993). *Teaching kids to spell*. Portsmouth, NH: Heinemann.

Goodman, K. (1967). Reading: A psycholinguistic guessing game. *Journal of the Reading Specialist, 6*, 126–135.

Goodman, K. (1973). *Theoretically based studies of patterns of miscues in oral reading performance*. Detroit, MI: Wayne State University. (ERIC ED 079 708)

Goodman, K. (1986). *What's whole in whole language?* Richmond Hill, ON: Scholastic.

Goodman, K., & Goodman, Y. (1990). Vygotsky in a whole-language perspective. In L. Moll (Ed.). *Vygotsky and education: Instructional implications and applications of sociohistorical psychology* (pp. 223–250). Cambridge, UK: Cambridge University Press.

Goodman, K., Goodman, Y., & Hood, W. (1989). *The whole language evaluation book*. Portsmouth, NH: Heinemann.

Goodman, Y. (1978). Kidwatching: An alternative to testing. *Journal of National Elementary School Principals, 57*, 22–27.

Goodman, Y., & Burke, C. (1972). *Reading miscue inventory manual: Procedure for diagnosis and evaluation*. New York: Macmillan.

Goodman, Y., & Marek, A. (1996). *Retrospective miscue analysis: Revaluing readers and reading*. Katonah, NY: Richard C. Owen.

Goodman, Y., Watson, D., & Burke, C. (1987). *Reading miscue inventory: Alternative procedures*. Katonah, NY: Richard C. Owen.

Graves, D. (1992). Portfolios: Keep a good idea growing. In D. Graves & B. Sunstein (Eds.), *Portfolio portraits* (pp. 1–12). Portsmouth, NH: Heinemann.

Green, A., & Lane, B. (Eds.). (1994). *The portfolio source book*. Shoreham, VT: Vermont Portfolio Institute.

Halliday, M. (1975). *Learning how to mean: Explorations in the development of language*. London: Elsevier.

Hansen, J. (1998). *When learners evaluate*. Portsmouth, NH: Heinemann.

Harp, B. (1996). *The handbook of literacy assessment and evaluation*. Norwood, MA: Christopher-Gordon.

Harwayne, S. (1993). *Lasting impressions: Weaving literature into the writing workshop*. Portsmouth, NH: Heinemann.

Heath, S. (1983). *Ways with words: Language life and work in communities and classrooms*. New York: Cambridge University Press.

Hill, B., & Ruptic, C. (1994). *Practical aspects of authentic assessment: Putting the pieces together*. Norwood, MA: Christopher-Gordon.

Holdaway, D. (1979). *The foundations of literacy*. Sydney, Australia: Ashton Scholastic.

Holland, K., Bloome, D., & Solsken, J. (Eds.). (1994). *Alternative perspectives in assessing children's language and literacy*. Norwood, NJ: Ablex.

Holloway, K. (1994). Language, culture and the implications of assessment. In K. Holland, D. Bloome, & J. Solsken (Eds.), *Alternative perspectives in assessing children's language and literacy* (pp. 11–20). Norwood, NJ: Ablex.

Jennings, M. (1994). Assessment in my world. In K. Holland, D. Bloome, & J. Solsken (Eds.), *Alternative perspectives in assessing children's language and literacy* (pp. 89–95). Norwood, NJ: Ablex.

Johnson, P. (1992). *Constructive evaluation of literate activity*. New York: Longman.

Juska, J. (1993). No more one-shots. In M.A. Smith & M. Ylvisaker (Eds.), *Teacher's voices: Portfolios in the classroom* (pp. 61–72). Berkeley, CA: National Writing Project.

Lovitt, T. (1989). *Introduction to learning disabilities*. Boston: Allyn & Bacon.

Milliken, M. (1992). A fifth-grade class uses portfolios. In *Portfolio portraits* (pp. 34–44). Portsmouth, NH: Heinemann.

Murphy, S., with Shannon, P., Johnston, P., & Hansen, J. (1998). *Fragile evidence: A critique of reading assessment*. Mahwah, NJ: Erlbaum.

Ninio, A., & Bruner, J. (1978). The achievement and antecedents of labeling. *Journal of Child Language, 5*, 1–15.

O'Keefe, T. (1996). Teachers as kidwatchers. In K. Short, J. Harste, & C. Burke (Eds.), *Creating classrooms for authors and inquirers* (2nd ed.). Portsmouth, NH: Heinemann.

Paley, V. (1984). *Wally's stories*. Cambridge, MA: Harvard University Press.

Palincsar, A., & Brown, D. (1987). Enhancing instructional time through attention to metacognition. *Journal of Learning Disabilities, 20*, 66–75.

Phinney, M. (1988). *Reading with the troubled reader*. Portsmouth, NH: Heinemann.

Piaget, J. (1955). *The language and thought of the child*. (M. Gabain, Trans.). New York: New American Library.

Porter, C., & Cleland, J. (1995). *The portfolio as a learning strategy*. Portsmouth, NH: Heinemann.

Power, B.M. (1996). *Taking note: Improving your observational notetaking*. York, ME: Stenhouse.

Rief, L. (1992). Eighth grade: Finding the value in evaluation. In D. Graves & B. Sunstein (Eds.), *Portfolio portraits* (pp. 45–60). Portsmouth, NH: Heinemann.

Rhodes, L., & Dudley-Marling, C. (1996). *Readers and writers with a difference: A holistic approach to teaching struggling readers and writers* (2nd ed.). Portsmouth, NH: Heinemann.

Rhodes, L., & Shanklin, N. (1993). *Windows into literacy: Assessing learners K–8*. Portsmouth, NH: Heinemann.

Roller, C.M. (1997). *Variability not disability: Struggling readers in a workshop classroom*. Newark, DE: International Reading Association.

Romano, T. (1992). Multigenre research: One college senior. In D. Graves & B. Sunstein (Eds.), *Portfolio portraits* (pp. 146–157). Portsmouth, NH: Heinemann.

Simmons, J. (1992). Portfolios for large-scale assessment. In D. Graves & B. Sunstein (Eds.), *Portfolio portraits* (pp. 96–113). Portsmouth, NH: Heinemann.

Short, K.G., Harste, J.C., & Burke, C. (1996). *Creating classrooms for authors and inquirers* (2nd ed.). Portsmouth, NH: Heinemann.

Slaughter, H. (1994). Alternative language assessment: Communicating naturally with students in assessment contexts. In K. Holland, D. Bloome, & J. Solsken (Eds.), *Alternative perspectives in assessing children's language and literacy* (pp. 103–117). Norwood, NJ: Ablex.

Smith, F. (1988). *Understanding reading* (4th ed.). Hillsdale, NJ: Erlbaum.

Smith, F. (1997). *Reading without nonsense* (3rd ed.). New York: Teachers College Press.

Taberski, S. (2000). *On solid ground: Strategies for teaching reading K–3*. Portsmouth, NH: Heinemann.

Tavalin, F. (1993). Vermont writing portfolios. In M. Smith & M. Ylvisaker (Eds.), *Teacher's voices: Portfolios in the classroom* (pp. 137–144). Berkeley, CA: National Writing Project.

Taylor, D. (1983). *Family literacy: Young children learning to read and write*. Exeter, NH: Heinemann.

Teale, W. (1982). Toward a theory of how children learn to read and write naturally. *Language Arts, 59*, 550–570.

Tepper, N., & Costa, R. (1994). Making assessment a process. In K. Holland, D. Bloome, & J. Solsken (Eds.), *Alternative perspectives in assessing children's language and literacy* (pp. 157–161). Norwood, NJ: Ablex.

Tierney, R., Carter, M., & Desai, L. (1991). *Portfolio assessment in the reading writing classroom*. Norwood, MA: Christopher-Gordon.

Valencia, S., & Pearson, P.D. (1987). Reading assessment: Time for a change. *The Reading Teacher, 40*(8), 726–733.

Vygotsky, L.S. (1978). *Mind in society: The development of higher psychological processes* (M. Cole, V. John-Steiner, S. Scribner, & E. Souberman, Eds. and Trans.). Cambridge, MA: Harvard University Press. (Original work published 1934)

Vygotsky, L.S. (1986). *Thought and language* (A. Kozalin, Trans.). Cambridge, MA: MIT Press. (Original work published 1934)

Watrous, B., & Willett, J. (1994). Assessing students as members of a literate community. In K. Holland, D. Bloome, & J. Solsken (Eds.), *Alternative perspectives in assessing children's language and literacy* (pp. 73–88). Norwood, NJ: Ablex.

Weaver, C. (1994). *Reading process and practice: From socio-psycholinguistics to whole language* (2nd ed.). Portsmouth, NH: Heinemann.

Wilde, S. (2000). *Miscue analysis made easy: Building on students strengths*. Portsmouth, NH: Heinemann.

Wilson-Keenan, J. (1994). Assessing the written language abilities of beginning writers. In K. Holland, D. Bloome, & J. Solsken (Eds.), *Alternative perspectives in assessing children's language and literacy* (pp. 118–136). Norwood, NJ: Ablex.

Children's Books Cited

Armitage, R., & Armitage, D. (1992). *Harry hates shopping*. New York: Scholastic.

Begaye, L.S. (1993). *Building a bridge*. Flagstaff, AZ: Northland.

Blos, J. (1987). *Old Henry*. New York: William Morrow.

Carle, E. (1987). *A house for a Hermit Crab*. Saxonville, MA: Picture Book Studios.

Cooney, B. (1982). *Miss Rumphius*. New York: Puffin Books.

de Paola, T. (1979). *Oliver Button is a sissy*. New York: Harcourt Brace Jovanovich.

Fox, M. (1985). *Wilfrid Gordon McDonald Partridge*. New York: Kane/Miller.

Giff, P.R. (1984). *The Candy Corn Contest*. New York: Yearling.

Henkes, K. (1991). *Chrysanthemum*. New York: The Trumpet Club.

Kilborne, S. (1994). *Peach & Blue*. New York: Alfred A. Knopf.

Kline, S. (1988). *Horrible Harry in Room 2B*. New York: Scholastic.

Mahy, M., & McRae, R. (Illus.). (1998). *The robber pig and the ginger beer*. Auckland, New Zealand: Shortland.

Nobisso, J. (1990). *Grandma's scrapbook*. New York: Green Tiger Press.

Polacco, P. (1992). *Chicken Sunday*. New York: Philomel.

Rosenberg, L. (1993). *Monster Mama*. New York: The Trumpet Club.

Rylant, C. (1989). *Henry and Mudge and the Forever Sea*. New York: Bradbury Press.

Rylant, C. (1994). *Henry and Mudge and the careful cousin*. New York: Bradbury Press.

Semple, C., & Juer, J. (1988). *Pancakes for supper*. Hawthorn, Victoria, Australia: Mimosa Publications.

Steig, W. (1971). *Amos and Boris*. New York: Farrar, Straus & Giroux.

Surat, M.M. (1983). *Angel child, dragon child*. New York: Carnival Press.

Viorst, J. (1972). *Alexander and the terrible, horrible, no good, very bad day*. New York: Atheneum.

Yashima, T. (1965). *Crow boy*. New York: Scholastic.

Young, E. (1992). *Seven blind mice*. New York: Scholastic.

Index

Note: Page numbers followed by *f* indicate figures.

TEPPER, N., 4
TESTING: vs. assessment, 3–4
TIERNEY, R., 6–7

V–Z

VALENCIA, S., 1
VERBAL SCAFFOLDING, 44–45. *See also* scaffolding
VYGOTSKY, L.S., 3, 5–6, 40, 44–46, 56, 82
WATROUS, B., 2
WATSON, D., 2, 21, 25–26
WEAVER, C., 2
WHAT MY PORTFOLIO SHOWS ABOUT ME, 79, 109
WILDE, S., 1, 2, 26
WILFRED GORDON MCDONALD PARTRIDGE (FOX), 14
WILLETT, J., 2
WILSON-KEENAN, J., 2
WORD BANK REFLECTION, 79, 108
WRITING CHECKLIST, 33, 96–97
WRITING REFLECTIONS, 63–66, 64*f,* 65*f,* 104
ZONE OF PROXIMAL DEVELOPMENT, 6, 44–45